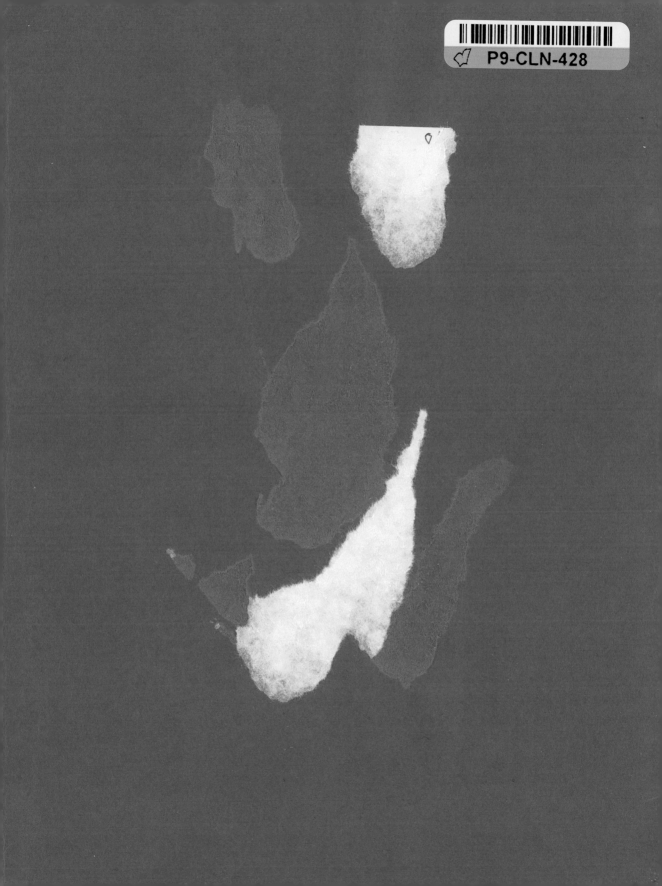

Knitting Know-How

Knitting Know-How

An Illustrated Encyclopedia

by Belle Meyers

illustrations by Phoebe Gaughan

HARPER & ROW, PUBLISHERS, New York
Cambridge, Hagerstown, Philadelphia, San Francisco,
London, Mexico City, São Paulo, Sydney

1817

746.9

FIRST EDITION

Designed by Suzanne Haldane

Library of Congress Cataloging
in Publication Data

Meyers, Belle.
   Knitting know-how.
1. Knitting. I. Title.
TT820.M499 1981   746.9′2   80–7857
ISBN 0–690–01954–8

81 82 83 84 85 10 9 8 7 6 5 4 3 2 1

B+T
8.97

*To all the people who want to knit—
especially those who feel they do not know
enough*
                    and
*to my husband, Murray, without whose
help, cooking, patience and prodding this
moment might not have been reached*
                    and
*to Carol Cohen, my editor, whose firm
hand and knowledge helped produce this
book.*

Introduction

The purpose of this book is to help anyone who wants to knit make lovely garments that can be worn with pride, that look handmade but not home-made. Through these pages I have tried to answer the questions that knitters frequently ask me, questions that have come up in the many years that I have taught people, not only how to knit, but also how to knit for proper fit.

The first thing I can tell you is not to be afraid. Knitting can be a very relaxing activity if you approach it with a relaxed attitude. This book tells you what you need to know about the techniques and fundamentals of knitting so that you can knit with confidence. With the help of this book you can make most of the things you like and make them well.

Not knowing how to read instructions is a common stumbling block for knitters. But more important, not knowing how to adapt instructions so that the knitted garment suits the one it is intended for stops many a knitter. They are puzzled by what to do with instructions written for someone of "average" height when they are knitting for someone who is taller than average. How do I change the sleeve length, a knitter may ask. Or knitters may want to change the style of the neckline or add sequins to a sweater and not know how. They may have seen some yarn that interested them in their yarn shop, but the garment in their instructions calls for a different weight yarn. How can I substitute the yarn I prefer, knitters often ask. By understanding the fundamentals and techniques of knitting and sizing explained in this book, the knitter can follow directions to make these changes with confidence and ease.

I always tell new knitters not to make a scarf their first project. It looks like an easy way to start because there is no shaping involved. You just cast on the number of stitches you need and keep knitting until the scarf is as long as you want it. But such a project doesn't teach the knitter anything except patience—it takes a long time to finish a scarf. So, instead I advise knitters to begin with a simple garment such as a sleeveless or classic sweater. You can make it in a short time and you can wear it right away. Nothing will more readily convince you that you can knit, and knit well, than being able, immediately, to wear what you've just made.

Decide on the way you want this sweater to look and when it will be worn. Do you want a lightweight sweater to wear under a suit jacket, a bulky sweater to go over a shirt? Learn how to measure, how to select yarn, make a gauge. Then go ahead.

Use your imagination to create garments of your own design. Once you understand the fundamentals, you can feel free to experiment with design, copy a design you like, combine yarns for different effects. Just remember—knitting is easy; all you need is information and, when necessary, a little arithmetic. The information is in this book. The arithmetic is the kind you use every day.

I have included in this book, in alphabetical order, all the knitting topics I could think of that would provide answers to the questions knitters have. And I have explained these topics as simply as possible. I might have missed a few things, or there may be something you'd like to know about that I haven't included. Let me know. Write to me in care of my publisher, Harper & Row.

But just remember: all you need to begin is a pair of needles and some yarn, and all you need to know is how to make a knit stitch and a purl stitch and this encyclopedia of knitting know-how.

Belle Bailynson Meyers

Knitting Know-How

Abbreviations and Symbols

Here are the abbreviations and symbols commonly found in knitting instructions. (However, for ease of reading, knitting terms are spelled out, not abbreviated, in this book.) For explanations of common terms used in knitting and found in instructions, see under INSTRUCTIONS. Although some abbreviations more commonly found in knitting instructions from England are included below, for a list of English knitting terms, their abbreviations, and their equivalents in American knitting, see ENGLISH KNITTING TERMS.

Common Abbreviations

alt	alternately: every other row or every other pattern
approx	approximately: about, not exact
beg	begin(ning): start of row or pattern
bo	binding off (same as casting off)
CC	contrasting color
co	casting off (same as binding off)
cont	continue: keep on going, following the instructions given previously
dec	decrease: reduce by one or more stitches
dp	double pointed (needles)
foll	follow(ing)
g st	garter stitch: knit every row
in	inch
inc	increase: add one or more stitches
K (or k)	knit: front of stockinette stitch
k and p	knit and purl

K wise	slip a stitch from one needle to another as if to knit it
kbl	knit from back of loop
kfb	knit from back of next stitch
kpk	knit purl knit
LC	left cross
LH	left hand
LT	left twist
MC	main color
M 1	make one: increase the number of stitches by one
no	number
P (or p)	purl: back of stockinette stitch
P wise	slip a stitch from one needle to another as if to purl it
patt	pattern: design or stitch used
pfb	purl into front and back of next stitch
pfl	purl from back of loop
psso	pass slip stitch over knit stitch
RC	right cross
rem	remain(ing): the stitches or patterns left to be done
rep	repeat (usually the pattern)
rev st st	reversed stockinette stitch
RH	right hand
rnd	round (in circular knitting): equivalent to a row in knitting on straight needles
RT	right twist
skpo	slip 1, knit 1, pass slipped stitch over knit stitch
sl	slip: slip stitch from one needle to the other
sp	space
st	stitch

st st	stockinette stitch: right side of work, made of 1 row knit and 1 row purl
tbl	through back of loop
tog	together (usually used when knitting two stitches together)
wrh (or yrh)	wool around hook
wrn (or yrn)	wool around needle
ybk	yarn back of work
yfwd	yarn front of work
yo (or yon or yrn)	yarn over (needle)

Asterisks

* This is called an asterisk. In instructions, an asterisk is printed either at the beginning or at the beginning and end of the stitches that make up the pattern, like this:

*K6P2

or like this:

K6P2

The stitches after or between the asterisks are to be repeated across the row the number of times called for. In instructions, for example, you might see:

K6P2 repeat 4 times

or:

K6P2 4 times

This means: K6P2 K6P2 K6P2 K6P2.

You will find directions that say:

P2 *K6P2* 4 times

This means: Start the row with P2, then repeat K6P2 K6P2 K6P2 K6P2.

Other times your pattern will say:

K6P2 4 times ending with K6

This means: You will K6P2 K6P2 K6P2 K6P2 and then knit the last 6 stitches.

Brackets [ ] or Parentheses ( )

These symbols are used when instructions for more than one size are given together. The smallest size and the instructions for it generally precede the first symbol. When you start a garment, circle the size you intend to follow and note whether it is the first, second, third, or other stitch number. Then circle the number given in the corresponding place within the brackets or parentheses in the rest of the instructions.

Example (if you are making a size 12):

Size 8 [(10) (12) (14) (16)]
Cast on 80 [(84) (88) (92) (98)] stitches.
Knit even for 9 [(9) (9½) (10) (11)] inches.

Parentheses may be used in the instructions instead of asterisks to tell you which groups of stitches are to be repeated. Parentheses are also used within square brackets in Aran knitting to show that a group of stitches is repeated within a complicated pattern.

Adding On Stitches

A row in a knitted piece is extended by adding on stitches. For example, you might add on stitches when making a sleeve in one piece with the body of a sweater, or you might add on stitches for a pocket or a neckline. There are many ways to do this. The simplest way to add on stitches is merely to take the yarn

(already attached to the knitted piece), twist it into a loop, twist it again, and place it on the needle. Repeat for the number of stitches needed.

You can also add on stitches following the procedures described at Knitting On Stitches under CASTING ON.

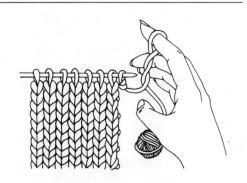

Adding on stitches

Afghans, Blankets, Carriage Covers, and Bed Covers

Afghans, blankets, and other covers can be made in strips or panels, which are then woven or crocheted together, or they can be knitted in one piece, using long circular needles.

First decide on the width needed. (See suggestions under specific covers below.)

Next decide whether you want to make the cover in sections (panels) or in one piece. Almost any pattern can be adjusted to be worked in panels. Figure out how many panels you need to fit the width you have decided upon. Make a gauge of the pattern you want to use (see GAUGE and STITCHES). Multiply the number of stitches to the inch by the number of inches in one panel. Use the closest number of stitches from your pattern stitch to fit the number required for the panel. When all the panels are made, you can join each section together by weaving or you can make a crochet or knit edge around each panel in the same or contrasting color. Add FRINGE if desired.

You can make the cover in one piece using a long circular needle, turning at the end of each row and working back and forth as if you were using straight needles. Again, make a gauge of the pattern stitch you want to use. Multiply the number of stitches to the inch by the number of inches needed. Use the closest number of stitches from your pattern stitch to fit the number of stitches needed. Cast on the stitches and work to the desired length. Use a crochet or knit edge for finishing, or add fringe.

You might want to make an afghan, blanket, or cover with a border all around. If you do, decide how wide you'd like this border and subtract twice its width from both the width and length of the cover you are planning.

Afghan

There are no standard sizes for afghans. You can make one to use as a small blanket to wrap around a baby or an adult or you can make a larger one that fits the top of a bed but does not hang down the sides.

Carriage Cover

For a carriage cover, measure the width of the carriage from one outer side edge to the opposite outer side edge and add 10 inches to this measurement. (This allows 5 inches on either side to tuck around the baby or to fall over the sides of the carriage.)

Measure the length from where the baby's neck will be to the bottom edge of the carriage, adding 5 inches for the fall over the bottom edge.

If you want to make a folded-over border near the baby's face, add it later instead of knitting it as part of the blanket. To do this, pick up the stitches of the finished cover, keeping the wrong side of the work facing you. Work the border so that the right side of the border is worked on top of the wrong side of the blanket. This way, when the border is folded over when finished, the right side of the border will be on top of the right side of the blanket.

Blanket or Bed Cover

Measure the width of the bed and add about 20 inches, so that you have a fall of 10 inches to drop over each side of the bed. Measure the length of the bed from the bottom of the pillow to the foot of the bed and add 10 inches for the fall there. If you prefer a cover that reaches the floor, measure the drop from the top of the mattress to the floor and add the necessary inches. If you want to cover the pillow, add 22 inches.

Altering Finished Knits

LENGTHENING and SHORTENING are dealt with under those headings. They are relatively simple operations, once you understand how to do them. But you may want to make a knit garment narrower or wider. Making knits narrower is not as simple as you may think. If the garment has been made on a circular needle and is one-piece, it can be made narrower or wider only if you are experienced at cutting knitted pieces and finishing off the cut edges so they won't unravel before making the alteration. I suggest taking the garment to a tailor experienced in altering knits if you have made a garment with no seams. If the garment is made in separate pieces, you can take in the seams at the sides if the shoulders do not need to be made narrower also. If the shoulders are too wide, take the garment to someone who knows how to alter knits. Don't attempt this kind of alteration yourself, unless you are experienced at it.

To make a garment narrower, open the side seams and the sleeve seams carefully, so as not to rip any stitches. Turn the garment inside out. Pin the side seams and the sleeve seams so that the garment will be the new and correct size. When pinning, graduate the new seam line to the original seam line at the point where

you are making no change. Weave the new side and sleeve seams along the lines you've pinned (see WEAVING). Then, with a simple basting stitch, sew down the old seam edges to the body of the garment and block, flattening the folded-back parts of the seam.

Widening a garment is simpler, if it is made in pieces and has side seams. Open the sleeve and side seams, being careful not to rip any of the stitches. If you have some of the same yarn, match the stitch and work a strip long enough to go up each side of the garment, under the arm, and down the sleeve to end at the wrist. Weave this insert piece in place (see WEAVING).

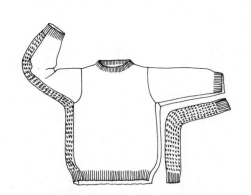

Making a sweater wider by adding inserts

If you do not have the same yarn, choose yarn similar in thickness but in a contrasting color. Using the same stitch or a different stitch, work up the insert strip and weave it into place. It might be fun to extend this new color into the garment you are widening, using DUPLI-CATE STITCH, if the style of the garment lends itself to this change.

Aran Knitting

Aran knitting is a combination of motifs on a purl background. The overall pattern created varies. Some of these patterns were designed by the knitters of the isle of Aran, an island off the coast of Ireland, where fishing is the principal industry. There is a tale that each family put together the motifs to make its own unique design for a sweater. Then sweaters were knitted for each family member, and each family was known by its particular sweater pattern. When a fisherman was hurt or died at sea, he could be identified by the sweater he wore. Traditional Aran sweaters are made with oiled (lanolin) waterproof yarn in a natural color.

An Aran sweater has a central panel, usually in a cable pattern. The panel can be wide or narrow, simple or complicated. On both sides of the center panel are vertical strips, usually 2 to 4 stitches each, with either a rib or purl section separating each strip. The side panels complete the design. They can be in the moss (or rice) stitch, a diamond pattern, a popcorn pattern, or a zigzag stitch.

To get a gauge for an Aran sweater, work up a swatch of each pattern (center panel, strips with their separating stitch-es, and side panel patterns). Measure each section across and add the measurements together. If you do not have enough stitches for the width you need, add additional stitches on the central panel by adding to the purl stitches on either side of the cable stitches, adding to the side panels, or adding to the strip patterns between center and side panels.

This is one sweater you can have fun with. You can combine patterns you like in any manner you like. Make sure you make a gauge of each pattern and combination of vertical strips and side panels. Allow sufficient width for a comfortable sweater. Aran sweaters should not be tightly fitted.

The best way to follow an Aran pattern is to keep each pattern separated from the next. This can best be done by placing MARKERS at the beginning and end of each pattern that is made of more than 2 stitches. Write each pattern on a 3-by-5-inch card. Then place and number the cards in the order you will knit them. As you read off the pattern row, turn the card face down. Do this with each card. Turn the cards face up and you are ready to start again. Here are some vertical patterns you can use:

Knotted Cord   This pattern can be made on a single stitch.

> ROW 1: Knit.
> ROW 2: Purl.
> ROW 3: Knit into the front of the stitch; leave the stitch on the needle. Knit the stitch from the back of the same stitch; leave the stitch on the needle. Knit this stitch from the front of the same stitch. Then knit

this stitch from the back.
ROW 4: Purl 4 stitches together.

Ring Cable Work this stitch over 8 stitches.

ROW 1: Knit 8.
ROW 2: Purl 8.
ROW 3: Slip the first 2 stitches onto a double-pointed cable needle and place in front of the work. Purl 2. Then knit 2 from the cable needle. Slip the next 2 stitches onto a cable needle and place in back of the work. Knit 2. Purl the 2 stitches from the cable needle.
ROW 4: Knit 2, purl 4, knit 2.
ROW 5: Purl 2, knit 4, purl 2.
ROW 6: Knit 2, purl 4, knit 2.
ROW 7: Slip the first 2 stitches onto a double-pointed cable needle and place in back of the work. Knit 2. Knit the 2 stitches from the cable needle. Slip 2 stitches onto the cable needle and place in front of the work. Knit 2. Knit the 2 stitches from the cable needle.
ROW 8: Purl 8.
Repeat these 8 rows for the pattern.

Single Zigzag A pattern worked over 8 stitches.

ROW 1: Purl 6. Skip the next stitch. Place needle into the front of second stitch and knit it. Leave it on the needle. Then purl the stitch you skipped; slip both stitches off the needle. This is called "cross two right," or "C2R."

ROW 2: Follow stitches from Row 1. This means knitting the stitches that were purled in row 1 and purling the stitches that were knit in row 1, or, in other words, working the stitch as it appears on the needle.
ROW 3: Purl 5. Skip the next stitch. Go into the following stitch and knit it. Leave it on your needle. Purl the stitch you skipped and drop both from the needle. Purl 1.
ROW 4: Repeat Row 2 on all even rows.
ROW 5: Purl 4, C2R, Purl 2.
ROW 7: Purl 3, C2R, purl 3.
ROW 9: Purl 2, C2R, purl 4.
ROW 11: Purl 1, C2R, purl 5.
ROW 13: C2R, purl 6.
ROW 15: Place the needle into the second stitch on the left-hand needle through the back of the stitch and purl it. Knit the first stitch and slip both off needle. This is called a "cross two left" or "C2L." Purl 6.
ROW 17: Purl 1, C2L, purl 5.
ROW 19: Purl 2, C2L, purl 4.
ROW 21: Purl 3, C2L, purl 3.
ROW 23: Purl 4, C2L, purl 2.
ROW 25: Purl 5, C2L, purl 1.
ROW 27: Purl 6, C2L.
ROW 29: Purl 1, knit 7.
ROW 30: Same as Row 2.
Repeat these 30 rows for one complete pattern.

Garter Rib   A pattern worked over 3 stitches.

ROW 1: Knit the first stitch going through the back of the loop. Knitting a stitch this way is referred to as TBL. Purl 1, knit 1 TBL.

ROW 2: Purl 3.

Repeat these 2 rows for the pattern.

Bobbles or Popcorn Stitch   This stitch, which stands out from the surface and looks like a small ball, is worked on 1 stitch, as follows:

Knit into the back and the front of the same stitch 3 times. You will have 6 stitches on the right-hand needle. Place the left-hand needle into the front of the second stitch in from the point of the needle and pull it over the first stitch. Next, pull the next stitch over the first stitch. Repeat until all stitches are pulled over and one stitch remains.

Allow at least 4 rows between bobbles. You can make a larger bobble or popcorn by increasing the number of times you knit into the same stitch.

Crossed Stitches   Work this pattern on 2 stitches.

ROW 1: Skip the first stitch on left-hand needle and go into the second stitch. Knit it and leave it on the needle. Then knit the first stitch and drop both stitches you knitted into from the left-hand needle.

ROW 2: With the right-hand needle in front of the work, skip the first stitch on the left-hand needle. Go into the second and purl it. Leave it on the needle. Then purl first stitch and drop both stitches you knitted into from the left-hand needle.

Repeat these 2 rows for pattern.

Argyle Designs

See under COLORS, CHANGING

Baby and Children's Sweaters

The measurements of most children from infancy until about 5 years of age are pretty similar. A 3-month child usually measures between 22 and 24 inches around the waist. This seems a lot for a tiny baby, but you must remember that babies don't have waistlines that are narrower than their hips or chest. As a baby grows, this measurement remains the same, sometimes not only to five years but up to the teens. If this sounds strange, check it out. Take measurements of some children. It will prove an interesting experiment.

Now, if the width of a child's sweater remains more or less the same, the only dimensions we must be sure of are the length of the armhole and the length of the garment from the underarm down. Both measurements depend not so much on how old the child is, but how tall.

If you are making a sweater for a child who is not living near enough to you so that you can take measurements, here are safe figures to use.

	Length in Inches	
Age	*Armhole*	*Sleeve (to underarm)*
3 to 12 months	3–4	6–8
1 to 3 years	4–4¾	8–9
3 to 5 years	4¾–5¼	9–10
5 to 10 years	5¼–6	10–11
10 to 13 years	6–7	*

*These are years of rapid growth. It's best to measure the child for sleeve length.

If the child is chubby, I advise taking measurements. Somehow, grandparents see their grandchildren as either very tiny or very big, depending on how they want to think of them. And some people knit baby and children's clothes too large so the child can grow into them. Children's knitted garments should not be big and baggy, and a sweater should not wrap around like a bathrobe.

Baby things can be made to look very delicate and tiny or bulky and large, in pale pastels or strong colors. Personally, I prefer strong colors. Have you ever seen a baby reach for a pale pink or blue or yellow blanket? But put a bright red, orange, yellow, or royal blue blanket in the crib and watch the reaction. The strong color catches the eye, and the baby's hand usually goes right out to it.

The first sweaters you knit for a baby should be practical ones. Then, when the child has enough sweaters, you can make more unusual ones. A sweater closed with ties is easiest to put on a tiny

squirmy infant. Sweaters with zippers instead of buttons are also quick to put on. A simple basic sweater for a young baby, then, would be one that ties or closes with a zipper.

Here are instructions for an easy first baby sweater. It is worked in a garter stitch (knitting every stitch, no purling). Knitting worsted is the most practical yarn for this sweater.

BACK: Using a 24-inch width and a gauge of 4 stitches to the inch, cast on 96 stitches. Work to length desired to underarm. Add on 32 stitches for one sleeve at the end of the last row (see ADDING ON STITCHES). Turn and knit across. Add on 32 stitches at the end of the second row for the other sleeve. Work 3½ inches on the 160 stitches. Knit 73 and cast off the next 14 stitches. Knit the next 73 stitches. These 14 stitches are the center of the back and allow about 3½ inches for the back of the neck.

FRONT: Working on one front at a time, work 1 inch on the 73 stitches. Cast on 9

Baby sweater closed with ties

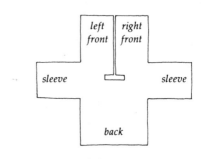

One-piece layout of baby sweater

stitches at center front (for front of neck). Work 2½ inches to finish the sleeve. Cast off the 32 sleeve stitches. Work remainder of front down to match the length of the back to bottom. (When measuring the front to match the back, make sure to place the 9 stitches you cast on for the center front 1 inch below the 14 stitches you cast off for the center back.) Break yarn. Connect yarn to other shoulder (at the beginning of the cast-off stitches for the neck). Work to correspond with the other front. Make sure you cast on the 9 stitches for the neck at center front and begin the casting off for the sleeve from end of sleeve. You can, if you wish, work both fronts at the same time, using two balls of wool. I recommend working one front at a time so that you avoid tangling the balls of yarn as you work. However, the choice is up to you.

NECK BAND: Using needles one size smaller than you used for the body of the sweater, and keeping the right side of the sweater facing you, pick up 36 stitches for a band around the neck, as follows: Connect the yarn in the first stitch in the top corner of the right front and pick up 1 stitch in every cast-on stitch. This means you have picked up 9 stitches. Pick up 2 stitches on right side of neck, 14 stitches at back of neck, 2 stitches at left side of neck, and 9 stitches across remaining cast-on stitches. Knit 1, purl 1 for 3 rows. Cast off loosely. If you cast off too tightly, the sweater will not go around the child's neck.

FINISHING: To finish the sweater, weave up the side seams and make ties to close the front. If you can crochet, pull your yarn through the top right corner of the right front, where you connected the yarn for the ribbing. Make a loop and chain 12 inches. Finish off. Do the same thing on the top left corner. On the front edge, at a point 3½ inches down from where the first chain is attached, make another chain on the right front and one on the left front.

If you cannot crochet, buy 1½ yards of ½-inch-wide ribbon. Cut it into four equal lengths. Sew one length to the top right corner, one to the top left corner, and one 3½ inches down on each of the fronts. Use the ribbons or crocheted chains to tie the sweater together.

Instead of ties, you can use a zipper to close a child's sweater. To measure for the zipper, lay the sweater down flat, being careful not to stretch the front edge. Place a tape measure along the edge and measure the length. Subtract ½ inch from this measurement. This allows for a ¼-inch space at the top and bottom of the zipper when it is sewn in place. Go to your notion, department, or yarn store and buy a separating zipper (one that completely opens at the bottom) which matches your yarn. If you cannot find a separating zipper in the right size, many stores will cut one for you. Pin the zipper into place ⅛ inch in from the edge of the sweater. Using matching sewing thread, sew down the outer edge of the zipper to the sweater. Next, do a running backstitch along the sewing lines marked on the zipper. If there are no marks on your zipper, do this stitch about ⅛ inch from the zipper teeth.

Beads

Beads are placed at intervals in a knitted item to form an overall pattern or design. They are knitted onto the top surface of the garment, not between the stitches.

When choosing beads, make sure the hole in the bead is large enough for the yarn you are planning to use to go through. Make sure the head of the needle you are going to use to string the beads onto the yarn is small enough to fit through the bead. If you are planning to knit with fine- or medium-weight yarn, thread the yarn through the eye of the needle and transfer the beads to the yarn by putting them on the needle, one at a time, and pulling them onto the yarn. If you are planning to use a heavy yarn, take a strand of sewing thread, fold it in half, and put both ends of the thread through the eye of the needle. Pull the end of the yarn through the loop at the end of the thread. Then string the beads from the needle onto the thread and *then* onto the yarn.

When knitting in stockinette stitch, the beads are worked in from the purl side. They will fall into place on the front of the knitting. If they don't, push them to the front. If you are using another stitch, work the beads in when you are working on the wrong side. Work the first stitch, slip a bead close to the garment, and purl the next stitch. Work until you are ready to use the next bead, then draw it close to the body of the garment and purl the next stitch. Repeat wherever you want to place a bead. Make sure you control the yarn so that the bead stays in place. There should be no loose stitches or excess yarn where the bead has been added.

If you wish to have a loop of beads instead of using a single bead in one stitch, push as many beads as you wish to form the loop close to the body of the garment and work the next stitch. Once again, control the yarn to make sure you do not get loose, dangling beads.

Belts

You can make a belt out of any yarn you like. It can match or contrast with your dress, sweater, or coat and can be worn at the waist or a little lower, on the top of the hip.

Braided Belt

Decide how long you want your belt to be, including the ties that hang down below the knot. Allow 2 extra inches for the knot.

For a braided belt, cut the strands of yarn 1½ times the desired length you want your finished belt to be. If you are using thick yarn, cut 9 lengths; with medium-weight yarn, cut 12 lengths; with thin yarn, cut 18 lengths. Knot the cut strands together about 5 inches from one end. Either ask someone to hold the knot or, using a heavy needle or a large pin, fasten the knot to the arm of a chair or to a rug. Separate the strands into three groups. (If you are using thick yarn, each group will have 3 strands; medium yarn, 4 strands each; thin yarn, 6 strands each.)

Braiding a belt

Holding the center group of strands in your left hand, take the strands on the right side in your right hand and place them over the center strands. Take the remaining strands in the left hand and place them over the combined strands in the center. Continue in this manner until the belt has as much braid as you wish. Make a knot. Cut, leaving the same length of loose strands (fringe) as at the beginning.

Double or Tubular Belt

Decide on the width of the belt you want. Cast on an even number of stitches equal to the width of the belt.

R O W 1: Knit.

R O W 2: Knit 2 stitches,*place the needle into the next stitch to knit, wrap yarn around the needle two times, then complete knitting the stitch. Bring yarn to front of work as if you were going to purl, slip the next stitch as if to purl*. Repeat the pattern between asterisks up to the last 2 stitches. Knit the last 2 stitches.

R O W 3: Knit 2 stitches, *start to knit the next stitch, wrap yarn around needle two times, complete knitting the stitch. Bring yarn to front of work, slip the next stitch (which is the stitch you made by wrapping the yarn around the needle twice) as if you were going to purl*. End by knitting the last 2 stitches.

Repeat row 3 for the desired length of the belt and cast off.

Knitted Ribbed Belt

Decide how wide you would like the belt to be. Cast on the number of stitches you would need for this width. You must cast on an odd number of stitches so that you begin and end with a knit stitch, making both edges of the belt match. For the first row, knit 1, purl 1 across the row, ending with a knit stitch. For the second row purl 1, knit 1, ending with a purl stitch. Repeat these 2 rows for the desired length of the belt.

Garter-stitch Belt

Work the same as ribbed belt, using the garter stitch.

Rope Belt

Decide how thick you want the rope belt to be. The number of strands of yarn you will use depends on the thickness of the yarn and the thickness of the rope belt desired. Rope belts are made by twisting yarn until it starts to buckle and then folding the twisted yarn in half and knotting. So when you calculate the thickness of the rope belt, take into account that your finished belt will be twice as thick as the yarn you twist together.

Cut yarn to three times the length of the rope belt you want. Knot the lengths together at each end, leaving enough for fringe. It will be simpler to work the cord with someone else's help. Each of you take a knitting needle, a pencil, or a stick of wood. Place this inside the knots, one at each end. Then each person begins turning the yarn to the right until the belt is tightly twisted. Pull tightly and fold in half. Knot the two ends together. Holding the knotted ends together, shake the rope, smooth it out, then make a knot at other end. Cut the loops and tease out the fringe. You now have one end with one knot and fringe and another end with two knots and fringe. You can either carefully untie the two knots that are now at one end and retie them together in only one knot or take a short strand of yarn (a simpler thing to do) and tie it above the two knots, tying them together.

Bias Knitting

See HERRINGBONE PATTERN

Binding Off

See CASTING OFF

Blankets

See AFGHANS, BLANKETS, CARRIAGE COVERS, AND BED COVERS

Blocking

There are all kinds of methods for blocking. Mine does not follow most of them, but it works. Try it. A garment made to the correct measurements (which allow for stretching when blocking so the garment will fit properly) does not have to be reblocked when it is washed.

Enlarging You've just finished a sweater. You try it on. It fits like the skin on a sausage. Is it made of wool or cotton? Don't give it away; these yarns can be manipulated and blocked. Acrylics, polyesters, and other synthetics usually cannot. If you read the labels on synthetics, they will tell you that synthetics must be worked to size only.

Back to the wool or cotton sweater. Turn on the cold water in your shower. Holding the sweater at the neck end, rapidly shake it back and forth under the spray—don't soak it, just dampen it. Roll it up. Take a board about 3 feet square. Place a cloth used for steaming, an ironing board cover, or a terry towel over the board. Set your iron to the steam/wool position. Lay the sweater out on the board.

Measure across the chest or bust. Suppose it measures 15 inches (which is 30 inches around). You feel you need at least 1 more inch across (2 inches around). Put both hands inside the sweater (which is still damp) and push it out by pulling your arms apart at the bust line or widest part of the chest and a little below. Do not pull the stitches at the borders. Take your hands out of the sweater. Measure again. Let us say this time it measures 15½ inches. You still need at least another ½ inch. Take a second terry towel, wet it in cold water, and wring it out. Place the wet towel, opened, on the sweater. With a steam iron, press down on the area you want to stretch. The iron will give off a sizzling sound. Keep the iron there for about 5 seconds. Move to the next area and do the same. Repeat until the entire area you want to stretch has been covered. Remove the towel.

Place your hands flat on the center of the area to be stretched and, pressing down on the sweater, move the palms of your hands in an outward direction,

moving away from the center toward the sides. Measure again. Repeat if necessary, but keep measuring or you might make the sweater too wide.

Now measure the length. If the sweater is a little short, use the same motion you used for making the sweater wider, going down toward the border of the sweater.

Check the armhole length. Steam the armhole seams and top. Measure and stretch the armholes if necessary. Do the same thing with the sleeves. To make sure both sleeves are the same length and width, fold the sweater across from right to left so that one sleeve is over the other. Block to make them match, if necessary.

Place the wet towel over the sweater again and repeat the steaming process on the entire sweater. Remove the towel. Pat the steam out with the palms of your hands. Let the sweater lie for about five minutes. Then move it to a dry area and leave it there, flat, until the dampness is out of the garment.

Follow the same procedure for a skirt, taking measurements at the hip and in the length. Block the skirt 1 inch larger than the hip measurement and shape it with your hands so that this inch you are adding at the hips is proportionately distributed down the sides of the skirt.

When blocking a coat, allow 2 extra inches across the widest part of the back and 2 inches extra in the front, 1 inch on each side. You can, of course, block the fronts a couple of inches wider if you prefer a greater overlap in your coat, but it is better to have taken this into account when figuring out how many stitches you needed to cast on for the fronts of the coat.

Narrowing   If the garment you are blocking is too wide, steam it the same way, but instead of pulling the garment out, reverse and push it together, palming toward the center of the sweater.

This blocking will put the garment back into shape if it has been stretched, and it can also be used to make a knitted garment about 1 inch smaller, if it has been knitted too large. But if it has been knitted much larger than that, you cannot shrink it into place.

Boat Neckline

Usually the back of a neckline is higher than the front of a neckline, since a neckline curves from the back to a lower point at the base of the neck in front. However, a boat neckline is worked the same on the back of the garment as on the front, and the base of the neckline is the same distance from the bottom of the garment in both front and back. The shoulder seams of garments are usually 4 inches when the side of the neckline rests at the base of the neck. Boat necklines rest about 1½ inches from the side of the neck, so the number of stitches at the shoulder should equal 2½ inches.

Let us assume you are working with a gauge of 4 stitches to the inch. Work the back of your sweater or other garment to the shoulder. Cast off the shoulder

stitches. (With the gauge we are using, this means you will cast off 10 stitches at each shoulder, always casting off from the beginning of the row.) Then cast off 2 more times at each side of the neckline. The first time cast off the number of stitches equal to 1 inch (for this example, 4 stitches). The second time cast off the number of stitches equal to 2 inches (8 stitches). Then cast off the remaining stitches. Work the front to correspond.

Sleeveless sweater with boat neckline

All the stitches you worked on and cast off after casting off for the shoulder will be folded back to the insides of the neckline to make the boat neck. Fold them in, making sure the folded pieces are flat, and fasten the edges to the insides by WEAVING. You might prefer folding the front part so that it is a little lower than the back.

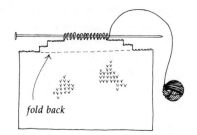

Boat neckline

Bobbins

See under EQUIPMENT

Borders

Borders are usually made in a different stitch from that used in the body of the knitted garment. Ribbing on a sweater can be called a border. Cuffs on a sweater or jacket can be called a border. Many different patterns or stitches can be used. The more experienced you become as a knitter, the more you will vary the borders you use and the more you will add borders to simple knits to make them distinctive.

For some simple borders, see Unstructured Hems or Borders under HEMS. For borders to add to the front edges of a cardigan, see CARDIGANS.

Buttonholes

Buttonholes are used in knitting for decoration or as a means of closing a sweater or jacket. In more expensive knitted garments the buttonholes are usually worked horizontally. Horizontally worked buttonholes do not pull or gap as easily as vertically worked buttonholes, but in many places where a narrow border is used, it is more practical to use a vertically worked buttonhole. *Remember:* Buttonholes for a woman's garment are worked on the right front and those for a man's garment are worked on the left front.

You can either work the buttonholes first and then find a button to fit, or you can fit the buttonhole to the buttons you plan to use. However, you must decide in advance whether the buttonholes are to be made on a border that is knitted as part of your garment or whether you are going to pick up stitches along the edge of the garment after the body is finished to make a border or edge for the buttonholes. You must also decide how many buttonholes you want.

Buttonholes should be evenly spaced. To show you how to divide the space evenly, let us take an example using 4 buttons on a sweater opening of 9 inches. Allow at least ¼ inch from the bottom edge of the sweater to the first buttonhole. You must also allow ¼ inch at the top. This leaves 8½ inches for the remaining 2 buttons in the example sweater.

Although you need only 2 more buttonholes, you need 3 spaces between

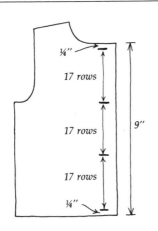

Spacing buttonholes

them. Dividing 8½ inches by 3 may be a mathematical problem you do not need. An easier way to find out where the remaining buttonholes go is to multiply the 8½ inches by the number of rows to the inch as determined by the GAUGE you worked before you started your project. Let's use 6 rows to the inch as our gauge in the example. Multiplying 8½ by 6 gives you 51 rows. Dividing 51 rows by 3 (the number of spaces needed) gives 17. So you now know that your buttonholes will be spaced 17 rows apart, and you also know that you will start the first buttonhole ¼ inch from the bottom of the sweater. When counting these 17 rows between buttonholes, count the row you start the buttonhole on as the first row. It will take more than 1 row to

complete a buttonhole, but do your counting starting where you have cast off or done a yarn-over stitch for the first buttonhole to the place where you will cast off again or do another yarn-over stitch again for the next buttonhole. Don't count from the top or the center of the buttonhole for these measurements.

Vertical Buttonhole

For a small button, make a vertical buttonhole just as you would make a horizontal one over 3 or 4 stitches. For a larger button, work as follows:

1. Determine where you want the buttonhole to be placed. For this example, we will assume that you have a 4-stitch border and you want the buttonhole to be placed 2 stitches in from the edge. Knit the first 2 stitches, turn, and work back. Turn. Slip these 2 stitches to the right-hand needle.
2. Break the yarn and connect it to the third stitch on the row. This is the first stitch on the left-hand needle. Work the remainder of the row. Turn and work back to the buttonhole space. Break the yarn.
3. Connect the yarn at the beginning of the knit row and work across the row, working across the buttonhole space.

If you need a larger buttonhole, work 3 rows on the first 2 stitches, instead of 2 rows, and 3 rows on the rest of the garment. Connect on the fourth row.

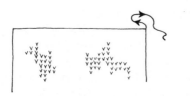

step 1

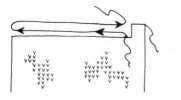

step 2

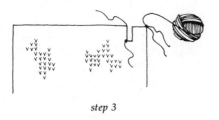

step 3

Making a vertical buttonhole

are making the buttonhole at the end of the row, work to the last 3 stitches, knit 2 together, yarn over, knit 1.

Creating a small buttonhole with a yarn-over stitch: the row being worked in the drawing shows knit 1, yarn over, knit 2 together

2. On the next row work the yarn-over as a stitch. The yarn-over stitch creates a small hole, which is the buttonhole.

Horizontal Buttonhole

A buttonhole for a small button can be worked over either 3 or 4 stitches. For a buttonhole made over 3 stitches, work as follows:

1. If you are making the buttonhole at the beginning of the row, knit 1, yarn over, knit 2 together. If you

Working the yarn over as a stitch

For a buttonhole made over 4 stitches, work as follows:

1. For a buttonhole at the beginning of the row, knit 2, yarn over, knit 2 together. If the buttonhole is placed at the end of the row, work to the last 4 stitches, knit 2 together, yarn over, knit 2.
2. On the next row work the yarn-over as a stitch.

For a larger button make a 5-stitch buttonhole, working as follows:

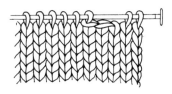

Horizontal buttonhole made with 5 stitches

1. If the buttonhole is made at the beginning of the row, knit 2, cast off 2, work the rest of the row. If made at the end of the row, work to the last 4 stitches, cast off 2 and knit 2.
2. On the next row add on 2 stitches right over the cast-off stitches by looping 2 stitches on needle (see ADDING ON STITCHES). Finish row.

Machine-made Buttonhole

Buttonholes can be made by machine after the garment is finished. Take them to a buttonhole maker. Don't try to do them on your home sewing machine. In most cases, buttonhole makers will insist that you sew on a strip of grosgrain ribbon as a backing for the machine stitching. When you buy the grosgrain, try to match it as closely as possible to the color of your garment. You will need a length a few inches longer than your garment opening and no wider than the border or edge. Preshrink the ribbon by washing it in hot water to ensure that it will not shrink when you wash your garment and cause puckers in the opening. Cut the ribbon so that it is ½ inch longer than the opening. Fold back ¼ inch at each end. Pin the strip on the inside (on the right side for a woman's garment, on the left side for a man's), just below the top edge to just above the bottom edge. Pin in place ⅛ inch in from the long edge. With matching thread, sew the ribbon down along both sides. Use pins to mark where you want the buttonholes. For a horizontal buttonhole, place pins across the ribbon. For a vertical buttonhole, place the pins going up and down in the center of the ribbon. You must remember that the buttonhole maker will sew the buttonholes wherever you place the pins. If you do not place the pins properly, your buttonholes will not be evenly spaced.

Cables

Cables are very decorative. They make an interesting pattern for sweaters, socks, dresses, coats, scarves, and even afghans and blankets. They are particularly noted in Aran knits. Cables are made by crossing a given number of stitches over the same number of stitches using a double-pointed cable needle (see NEEDLES). Cables made of knit stitches usually are worked with purl stitches on either side of the cable. These purl stitches emphasize the cable, making it stand out from the surface of the knitting. However, cables can also be made without these purl stitches at either side.

Single Cable Cables can be made with as few as 4 stitches. To cross 4 stitches into a cable:

1. Slip the first 2 stitches onto a double-pointed cable needle and place the needle and the stitches at the back of the garment.
2. Knit the next 2 stitches onto the right-hand needle.
3. Knit the 2 stitches from the cable needle to the right-hand needle.

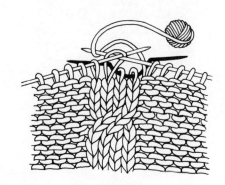

Single cable crossing to the right

This will make a cable that crosses to the right. If you prefer a cable crossing to the left:

1. Slip the first 2 stitches onto the double-pointed cable needle and place them in front of the garment.
2. Knit the next 2 stitches from the left-hand needle to the right-hand needle.
3. Knit the 2 stitches from the cable needle to the right-hand needle.

The cable twist is spaced evenly, every fourth, sixth, eighth, or tenth row, depending on the depth of cable you prefer.

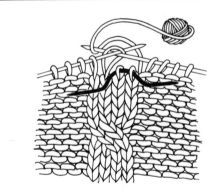

Single cable crossing to the left

Braided or Plaited Cable   This cable looks like a braid. It can be made by using a multiple of 2 stitches (6 stitches for the cable), 3 stitches (9 stitches for the cable), or 4 stitches (12 stitches for the cable). The same principle is used in making the cable, no matter how many stitches are in it.

Assume you are making a 9-stitch cable and you want each twist to be 1½ inches apart. With the knit side of the cable facing:

1. Slip the first 3 stitches onto a double-pointed cable needle and place in back of the work.
2. Knit the next 3 stitches.
3. Knit the stitches off the cable needle.
4. Knit the last 3 stitches.
5. Work 5 rows straight, without doing the cable. (This can be 7 rows or 9 rows or whatever distance you would like between the cables.)
6. Knit the first 3 stitches.
7. Slip the next 3 stitches onto a double-pointed cable needle and place in front of the work.
8. Knit the last 3 stitches.
9. Knit the 3 stitches off the cable needle.
10. Work the same number of rows between the cable twists as before and repeat from step 1.

Double Cable   A double cable is actually two cables, one right next to the other but each twisting in opposite directions. For example, for a cable made of a multiple of 12 stitches, there would be 6 stitches in the first cable and 6 stitches in the second cable. Work as follows:

1. Slip the first 3 stitches onto a double-pointed cable needle and place in back of the work.
2. Knit the next 3 stitches onto the right-hand needle.
3. Knit the 3 stitches from the cable needle onto the right-hand needle.
4. Slip the next 3 stitches onto the cable needle and place in front of the work.
5. Knit the next 3 stitches.
6. Knit the 3 stitches off the cable needle.
7. Work 4, 6, or 8 rows (or the amount of space you want between cables) and repeat.

Chain Cable   This cable looks like a rib and makes an interesting pattern. It can be made unevenly spaced—that is, the number of rows between the cable twist can vary. Use at least 2 purl stitches on either side of the cable and allow 6 stitches for the cable. (The number of purl stitches on either side of the cable can be varied, but do not use less than 2.) In the following example, 3 purl stitches are used on either side of the cable stitches.

ROW 1: Knit 3, purl 6, knit 3.
ROW 2: Purl 2. Slip the next stitch onto a double-pointed cable needle and place at the back of the work. Knit 3, then purl 1 stitch from the cable needle. Slip the next 3 stitches onto the cable needle and leave in the front of the work. Purl 1, then knit the 3 stitches from the cable needle. Purl 2.

ROW 3: Knit 2, purl 3, knit 2, purl 3, knit 2.

Follow the ribbing as established in Row 3 for the number of rows you want to have between the cable twists. For the cable twist, repeat Row 2.

Wavy Cable   Doing this cable requires 2 double-pointed cable needles. It is worked on 15 stitches, and the cable twists are made on every 16th row. The following directions are to be used when working on straight needles (or back and forth on circular needles).

ROW 1: Purl 3, knit 9, purl 3.
ROW 2: Knit 3, purl 9, knit 3.
ROW 3: Same as Row 1.
ROW 4: Same as Row 2.
ROW 5: Purl 3. Slip the next 3 stitches onto the first cable needle and place in the back of the work. Slip next 3 stitches on second cable needle and leave in front of work. Knit the next 3 stitches. Then knit 3 stitches from second cable needle (the needle in front of the work). Then knit 3 stitches from first cable needle (the needle in back of the work). Purl 3.

Work 15 rows alternating Rows 2 and 1 and repeat the cable as described for Row 5.

For circular needles working in the round:

Rounds 1, 2, 3, and 4: Purl 3, knit 9, purl 3.

Round 5: Follow directions for round 5 given for straight needles. Work 15 rounds repeating rounds 1 through 5, always cabling on the fifth round.

Casting Off a Cable

If your casting-off row comes at the same place as your cable-twist row, follow this procedure:

1. Slip the stitches to make the cable onto your cable needle, either in front or in back, as you have done for the entire garment.
2. Slip the remaining stitches for the cable onto the right-hand needle.
3. Place the stitches from the cable needle on the left-hand needle.
4. Place all the stitches for the cable that are now on the right-hand needle back onto the left-hand needle.
5. Proceed with the casting off.

Cable-stitch Needles

See under NEEDLES

Capes

A cape is made the same as a circular poncho except that it is open down the front.

Short Cape

Working from the Top   For a circular cape worked from the neck down, follow the procedure described under PONCHOS but work back and forth instead of in a circle. The finished cape should measure at least 120 inches across the bottom. When making the increases, do so evenly across the row, but do not make any increases along the front edges. You want the front edges to be straight; if you make any increases there, the edges will be slanted. Also, make sure you have the same number of stitches before the first increase and after the last increase. You do this increasing by knitting up to the stitch that is to be increased, knitting it, and then picking up a stitch *after* this stitch (see INCREASING). On the other front, knit up to the stitch that is to be increased, pick up the stitch to be added, knit it, and then knit the stitch on the needle. Work the cape even until the desired length. Cast off loosely. Finish off with a crocheted edge, a knit edge, or a border. See Edges under FINISHING, or see HEMS. For some borders to knit along the front opening, see under CARDIGANS.

You might want to add a small round collar to this cape. To do this, pick up the cape and, with the wrong side facing you, connect the yarn at the third stitch in from the front edge. This is the third stitch in the neckline. For a gauge of 7 stitches to 2 inches as described under PONCHOS, pick up about 44 stitches across the neck up to the third stitch from the end of the row. If you are working with a different gauge, starting from the third stitch in from the edge, pick up the number of stitches across the neckline equal to 12 inches. Purl back. On the next row increase 1 stitch in every third stitch across the row. Work even until the collar is as deep as you wish.

Working from the Bottom For a short circular cape worked from the bottom up, first determine the number of stitches necessary to make 120 inches. Divide this number by 4 to find out where to put your four markers for decreasing. You now need to know how many stitches make up each front. To find this number, divide one of the fourths by 2. If you can't divide by 2 evenly, either add or subtract 1 stitch. As an example, using the same gauge and dimensions as described under PONCHOS, let us use 420 stitches. Dividing this by 4 gives 105, the number of stitches in each section. Now divide the stitches of one section for the front. Since it is difficult to divide 105 in half, either cast on 1 more stitch to this panel, making 106 stitches, or cast on 1 less stitch, making the number 104. Let us use 106 stitches. Dividing this by 2 gives us 53 stitches for each front.

Cast on 421 stitches. Place a marker after the first 53 stitches; count 105 stitches and place another marker; count 105 stitches, place another marker; count 105 stitches, place the last marker. There are 53 stitches left. Decrease before and after each marker every other row until 53 stitches remain. Cast off. Finish off bottom and front edges following suggestions for cape worked from the neck down.

Long Cape

A long cape is usually made only slightly wider than a short cape. Of course, if you like a sweeping cape, add more inches to the bottom.

If you are working from the neck down, make the additional increases every 4 or 5 inches until you have the length and width you want.

If you are working from the bottom up, you must first decide how wide and how long you want the cape to be. The major decreasing is done in the top 12 inches, where the cape is shaped over the shoulder. The neck is usually 16 inches. Multiply the number of rows to the inch in your gauge by 12. This will give you the number of rows you have for shaping (decreasing) over the shoulder to the neck. Divide this number of rows by two, since you are going to decrease on the knit row only. I recommend decreasing 8 to 10 stitches in each knit row here. Why this amount? Well, if you were decreasing for a raglan, you would be decreasing 2 stitches at each of the four shoulder points, for a total of 8. This works up to the neck very nicely. A slightly more rapid decrease (which I would recommend) would be 10 stitches in every knit row.

Now that you know how many stitches you will decrease on the top 12 inches of the cape, you can figure how many stitches you will have to decrease from the bottom of the cape up to this point.

Subtract the number of stitches you have at the bottom of the cape from the number of stitches you will have at the 12-inch point. Divide the decreases so that you start your first decrease about 6 inches from the bottom and then decrease every 3 or 4 inches.

Making a Place for the Arms You can knit strips to be sewn to the inside of the cape to be used as rests for the arms. Slipping the arms into these strips also serves to keep the cape closer to the body and helps stop it from flying open. Strips have a disadvantage, though. With strips the only way you can reach anything when wearing the cape is through the center opening. Another way to make a place for the arms is to knit slits into the cape for the arms to go through.

STRIPS: Knit two strips about 2½ inches wide and 7 inches long. Try on the finished cape and bend your elbows. Mark the place where armrests would be most comfortable and sew one strip on the inside of each front at a point where it will hold the cape in place comfortably when your arms are slipped through.

SLITS: Work up (from the bottom) until the cape is 17 inches shorter than the length you intend to make it. The slit for the arms will begin at this point. Start the slit 5 inches from the edge. For this example, we'll use the same gauge as the preceding cape, 7 stitches to 2 inches (3½ stitches to the inch). Multiplying 3½ by 5 gives you 17½, rounded to 18. To start the slit, work the first 18 stitches from the edge. Work back and forth on these 18 stitches for 5 inches, ending with a knit row. Break the yarn.

Connect the yarn at the base of the slit and work up to the last 18 stitches at the end of your needle. Turn. Work back and forth until this center section is the same length as the first section, ending on a knit row. Break the yarn.

Connect the yarn to the eighteenth stitch in from the end of the needle. Work this section up to match the first two sections, ending with a knit row. Turn. Connect the sections by purling back across the entire cape (or following whatever pattern stitch you are using). Continue working the cape. Don't forget to make whatever decreases are necessary in the body of the cape while you are working these 5-inch sections for the slits.

Cardigans

A cardigan is a sweater or jacket that opens down the front. It can be fastened with buttons or with a zipper. Or it can be made to wear open, with no closings.

A cardigan is usually worn on top of something else, so it usually is made slightly larger than a pullover. If the cardigan is to be worn with a certain pullover, make the cardigan 1 to 1½ inches longer. Otherwise it can be any length. Unless you want a snug-fitting cardigan, allow at least 1 inch more for the front and 1 inch more for the back than you would for a pullover. If you plan to use buttons as a closing, allow extra inches for the overlap. The number of inches to add for the overlap depends on how wide you want this button border to be. You do not need the additional inches for a border if you are going to use a zipper closing, since there is no overlap.

To make a classic cardigan, read the classic sweater section under SWEATERS and add the necessary stitches as just described.

A V neck in a cardigan is made the same way as a V neck in a pullover. To figure out how and where to decrease, see V NECKLINE.

Borders for Cardigans

You can finish the edges of the cardigan using a slip stitch (see Edges under FINISHING). Or you can make a border.

Garter-Stitch (All-Knit) Border   Let us assume you want a 1-inch border and your gauge is 4 stitches to the inch. Make sure you cast on 4 extra stitches on each front. Start the border for the right front on the first row by knitting the first 4 stitches. On the next row, knit the last 4 stitches. Reverse this for the left front, by knitting the last 4 stitches on the first row and the first 4 stitches on the next row.

Moss or Seed-Stitch Border   This border is easier to work if you use an odd number of stitches. Follow the procedure described under Garter Stitch Border, working the border stitches in moss stitch (see under STITCHES) on the first row.

Rib-Stitch Border   This border is made a little differently. Work the ribbing at the bottom of the cardigan. On the next row, knit 1, purl 1 for the 6 border stitches. Place these on a thread. Continue ribbing for the rest of the row up to

the last 6 stitches. Place the last 6 stitches on a thread. Continue working the cardigan. When it is finished, place the first 6 stitches that are on the thread onto your needle. Using these 6 stitches and the same needle used for the bottom ribbing, make a strip of ribbing 1 inch shorter than the length of the front to allow for the fact that knitting made of garter stitch will stretch. Cast off. Weave this ribbed border to the edge of the cardigan. Repeat with the 6 last stitches on the other thread.

Added On Border   You can pick up the border for the cardigan after finishing the entire body of the sweater but before putting on the neck band. First measure the front edge to determine the number of stitches you need to pick up for the border, or add the number of inches you knitted up to the underarm to the number of inches you knitted up to the neck. Let us say you worked 12 inches to the underarm and 7½ inches up to the neck shaping. This totals 19½ inches. Assuming a gauge of 4 stitches to the inch, the number of stitches you pick up along the edge should be 19½ times 4, or 78. Pick these stitches up using a needle one or two sizes smaller than the one you used to knit the cardigan. For a ribbed edge, subtract 1 inch, or 4 stitches, from your total. When making a faced border, subtract 1½ inches, or 6 stitches, from the total. If you pick up the exact number of stitches, the facing will be bulky.

If you are making the cardigan on a circular needle with no side seams, you must remember, when dividing the stitches for the underarm, that the additional stitches on each front go to the front sections.

Shaping the armhole, neck, and shoulders for the cardigan is the same as for the pullover except that you must remember to cast off the extra border stitches on either front at the neck; that is, the number of stitches you were to cast off plus the number of the stitches on the borders.

When picking up stitches for the neck band, connect the yarn at the right-hand corner at the top of the right front with the right side of the cardigan facing you. Use the same needle as you did for the ribbing. Multiply the number of stitches to the inch (4 in this case) by 16, the number of inches around the neck. Pick up 64 stitches. Work in ribbing for 1 inch. Cast off following knit stitch over knit stitch and purl stitch over purl stitch.

Picking Up Stitches for Borders   When picking up stitches for a border down the front of a sweater, coat, or jacket, make sure that you pick up the same number of stitches on both fronts. To do this evenly, place a pin on the top and bottom of the edge that will have the border. Find the center of this edge and put a pin there. Place another pin between the top and center and still another pin between the bottom and the center pin. Divide the number of stitches you need to pick up on the first side by 4, and pick up that number of stitches between the pins of each section.

When making a border that you begin by picking up stitches, do not count the row of picked-up stitches as one of the rows needed to make the border. Also, do not count the cast-off row as one of the rows needed to make the border.

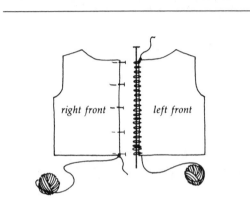

Picking up stitches on the right and left fronts of a cardigan

HOW TO PICK UP STITCHES: With the right side of the cardigan's right front facing you, connect the yarn to the lower corner. Go through the corner stitch with your knitting needle. Wrap the yarn around the needle by bringing the yarn under the needle and pulling it over the needle, and pull this strand of yarn through the space made by your needle. Continue picking up in this manner until you've picked up all the stitches you need. Wherever possible, go into the small nub at the edge of the row when pulling the stitch through. For additional stitches, you will have to pick up between the nubs.

Picking up stitches along the right front

Care of Knits

See WASHING, DRY CLEANING, and STORING KNITS.
Be sure to read the section on hanging knits on hangers under STORING KNITS.

Carriage Cover

See AFGHANS, BLANKETS, CARRIAGE COVERS, AND BED COVERS.

Casting Off

Casting off, sometimes called *binding off*, is the method by which you close off the top of a stitch so that it will not unravel when the needle is removed. This is how you end your knitted piece, but casting off is also used to shape a neckline, make a buttonhole, and form an underarm, among other things.

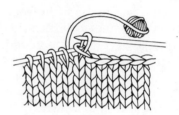

Casting off

To cast off, knit two stitches. With the left-hand needle pick up the first stitch and pass it over the second stitch. Drop this stitch. Knit the next stitch and repeat until you have cast off all the required stitches.

Another way to cast off is to knit the first two stitches together and then place this newly created stitch back on the left-hand needle. Repeat until all the stitches are cast off. Since this method can produce a tight cast-off row, I recommend that you use a larger needle to knit the 2 stitches together while casting off. Do not use this method when casting off ribbing, especially at the neck, since this method does not allow for much stretch in the finished row and it is essential to have as much stretch as possible in the neck so that it goes over the head easily.

Hint: Have you ever cast off a neck band very evenly and neatly, only to find that the neck opening will not go over your head? Or cast off the ribbed band on your cardigan, but when you tried it on it was too short in front? Or cast off on the top of a skirt and found it would not go over your shoulders?

You can avoid such problems by using a needle two sizes larger for your casting-off needle and making sure you do not pull the yarn for each stitch as you cast it off.

Be sure to cast off in the stitch you are working in. Don't switch to all knit stitches. For instance, if you are casting off a knit 1, purl 1 around the neck, you must knit 1, purl 1 as you cast off.

Casting Off for Yarns with No Stretch   You might have difficulty in the cast-off row when using yarns such as cotton and linen because such yarns have no stretch. Here is a typical example: The crew neck on the sweater you made will not go over your head no matter how loosely you have cast off, or it will go over your head but the cast-off stitches are so loose they look awful.

Cast off in the usual manner but (depending on how much more stretch you

need) increase an occasional stitch and cast this stitch off as you would a regular stitch.

Casting off yarn with no stretch

Try to judge how many inches you need to make the edge comfortable and neat. Multiply the number of inches you need by the number of stitches you get to the inch. Spacing the increases evenly apart, increase the needed stitches in the cast-off row.

To increase and cast off a stitch at the same time, cast off to the place where you want to make the increase. With the right-hand needle, pick up the back of the stitch to be increased and place it on the needle. Then cast it off. Continue to the next increase point.

Another way to increase is to double-loop an extra stitch onto the right-hand needle and then cast it off.

Casting Off a Cable   See under CABLES

Casting Off for Shoulder   When stitches are cast off for a shoulder, they usually are cast off at the beginning of a number of rows. This creates a steplike effect. There are two ways to soften the steps into a smooth line.

METHOD 1: Cast off the necessary stitches at the beginning of the first row. Finish the row. Work back. Turn. Instead of knitting the first stitch, slip it. Knit the next stitch and cast off as usual, pulling the slip stitch over the knit stitch.

METHOD 2: Cast off the necessary stitches at the beginning of the first row but don't work the last stitch on the row. Place it on the right-hand needle, turn, and proceed to cast off.

Casting On

Casting on is the placing of stitches on a knitting needle to begin or to enlarge a knitted piece. Casting on stitches to a knitted piece that is partially finished (such as adding stitches for a sleeve after the body of a sweater is worked) is also called *adding on.*

There are many ways to cast on, and each creates its own distinctive edge. Use the same method for all the pieces of a garment that has more than one piece. Make sure that the cast-on edge is always on the same side of the knitting; that is, either on the right side (the knit side) or the wrong side (the purl side), so that when the pieces are sewn together the edge stitches at the bottoms will match.

Single Cast

Make a loop and place it on the needle. Make a loop with the yarn, using your right hand, and twist the loop again. Slip the loop onto the left-hand needle. Continue until you have the required number of stitches. If you want a looser edge, follow the same procedure but cast onto two needles held together as if they were a single needle. The cast-on stitch will be a looser stitch when the extra needle is pulled out.

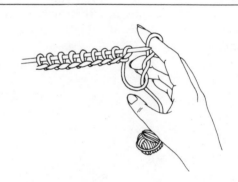

Single cast-on

Double Cast

Although the double-cast methods are more difficult to learn than the single cast, with practice you can soon cast on stitches automatically without thinking about all the steps involved.

Double cast-on methods begin with a loop made not at the end of the yarn but somewhere along the length of the yarn, and the stitches are cast on using two strands of yarn. For practice, start with the yarn at a point about 20 inches from the beginning of the ball. After you become experienced in double casting on, you will be able to judge how far from the end of the ball of yarn to begin. Here is a rough guide: Take the end of the yarn and draw it at arm's length from your nose or from the center of your chest (about a yard). This should cast on 25 stitches, using heavy yarn. The same length in medium yarn will cast on about 35 stitches; the same length of fine yarn will cast on about 45 to 50 stitches.

on your left thumb by going from left to right. Place this loop on the needle. Make another loop on the left thumb. Take the hanging strand of yarn and wrap it around the needle by going under the needle, bring it between thumb and needle, and knit this strand through the loop. Repeat until you have the number of stitches you need.
METHOD 2: Take the yarn you have measured off and place it over your thumb and then over your forefinger.

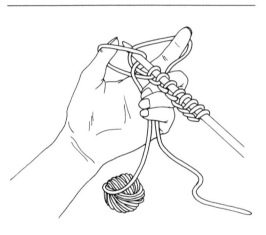

Double cast-on: method 2

Double cast-on: method 1

METHOD 1: Starting at a point 20 inches from the end of the yarn, make a loop

Fold the remaining fingers into the palm of your hand and grasp the end of the yarn hanging from the left side of your thumb and the end of yarn hanging from the right side of your forefinger. Take the needle in your right hand. With the needle, take the strip of yarn between your thumb and forefinger and pull it down toward your palm to form a V. Holding the yarn in this V position, take the needle and put it through the loop on your thumb. Reach across with the point of needle and catch the strand on outer side of forefinger. Pull it through loop on the thumb. Remove your thumb from the loop and adjust the yarn for stitch. Pull the yarn back into the V between thumb and forefinger. You now have one stitch on the needle. Proceed in the same way—placing the needle in the loop on the thumb, catching the yarn from the outer side of the forefinger, and pulling it through the loop—until all the stitches are cast on.

Knitting On

METHOD 1: Make a loop at the beginning of the strand and place it on the left-hand needle. Knit this stitch and place the knitted stitch back on the left-hand needle. Knit this stitch and place it back on the left-hand needle. Continue until you have the required number of stitches.

METHOD 2: This is like knitting on the stitches except that, instead of putting your right-hand needle through the loop on the left-hand needle, you work as follows: Make a loop on the left-hand needle. For the second cast-on stitch, go into the loop and knit through it. Place this stitch on the left-hand needle. Now this is the change: place the right-hand needle between the 2 stitches. Place yarn around the needle, going between the needles from underneath and over the top of the needle, and away from the needle. Pull the yarn through the space.

Place the stitch you just pulled through on the left-hand needle and knit it. Repeat for the desired number of stitches.

Knitting on stitches: method 2

Hint: You have cast on your stitches. You are now going to work off the first row. The tendency to make each stitch exact and even makes knitters pull the yarn between each stitch. If you do this, you will suddenly notice that you have a length of yarn between your needles that is getting longer all the time. There is no need for this to happen. To prevent it, when you work off your first row, just work each stitch and let it go onto the right-hand needle. *Do not* pull the yarn to make the stitch even.

Casting On for Yarns with No Stretch
Add 4 or 5 extra stitches on the cast-on row when you are working with yarn that has no stretch, such as linen or cotton, particularly when you are casting on the cuff of a sleeve or stitches at the

waist. Without these extra stitches you will find it difficult to pull your hand through the cuff of the sleeve or pull the garment down over the body. But you must eliminate these extra stitches on the very first row of knitting. Do this by DECREASING evenly across the row.

Children's Sweaters

See BABY AND CHILDREN'S SWEATERS

Colors, Changing

Horizontal Stripes

To change color when knitting horizontal stripes, work the first color, A, for the number of rows desired. Then attach the second color, B, by tying it around the strand of A. Do not break yarn A. Tie it firmly. Pull B up close to the needle and work for the desired number of rows. If you are making the next stripe of A, pick up A and raise it to the next row. Do not pull it tightly. Continue working. Repeat this for the number of stripes necessary.

If the stripes are wide (more than 4 rows) or if you are making stripes of many colors, I recommend breaking the yarn after knitting the stripe, especially if you are working with bulky yarn. If you prefer, you can carry the color to the next time you need it by twisting it every 4 rows with the colors you are using. If you decide to break the yarn and you are working on straight needles, leave an end long enough to sew that color stripe to its counterpart in the other parts of the garment, when appropriate. When using circular needles, you do not have to break the yarn if you do not mind the loop of yarn on the inside of your garment. If you think the loop of yarn is too long, cut it and leave a strand long enough to finish off on the inside.

Vertical Stripes

If you are planning vertical stripes of from 1 to 5 stitches, carry the yarn along the back or wrong side of the garment. This method of knitting is referred to as *looping,* or *stranding.* You must make sure to carry the thread behind the number of stitches at a normal tension so that it is neither too tight nor too loose. If you loop the yarn too tightly, the knitting will pull together and the stitches will pucker. If the yarn between the colors is too loose, it will hang and be likely to catch when the garment is put on. Hold the yarn so that the knitted piece falls naturally.

If you are carrying a color behind a larger number of stitches, weave the yarn through the back of the stitches you are passing. To weave, carry the second color that is to be carried behind the work in your left hand. Use your left hand to place this second color first above, then below, the stitch you are working on with the first color. Use your right hand to place the first color either above or below the stitch you are working on with your left hand. This sounds

into the next stitch to purl, bringing the yarn from left hand below the needle. Finish purling the stitch.

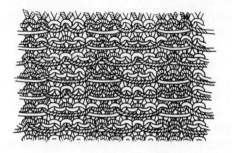

Wrong side of two-color knitted piece, showing yarn carried behind stitches (stranding)

Weaving colors

more complicated than it really is. Let us take it step by step.

1. Start by knitting a stitch with the first color with your right hand. Place your needle through the stitch you are going to knit. With the second color in your left hand, place the yarn across the top of the right-hand needle. Finish knitting your stitch so that the second color is caught behind the stitch.
2. Place your right-hand needle into the next stitch. Take the yarn from left hand and place it under the needle. Knit the stitch. Repeat this for the number of stitches needed for the first color.
3. Do the same thing on the purl row, only in reverse. Place the needle into the stitch to purl, bring the left-hand yarn up and across, purl the stitch, and bring the yarn down. For the next stitch, place the needle

Geometric or Abstract Designs

When knitting with more than one color to form abstract or geometric designs, intertwine the colors to avoid holes. To do this, cross the color you have finished

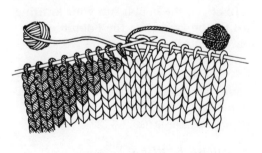

Changing colors in a geometric design

knitting above the new color, drop the first color, and begin knitting with the new color. Use a separate ball of yarn for each color.

If your geometric design includes a slant that leans to the right, such as you might have in an argyle pattern, loop the yarn on the knit side. It will fall into its proper place when you purl back on the next row, and you do not have to intertwine it again. When making a slant that leans to the left, interlock the yarns on the purl side. It will not be necessary to interlock the color on the knit side since it will fall into place there.

If your design calls for a vertical line, you must interlock the colors on every row.

Argyle Designs

When making an argyle design, it is best to use bobbins instead of carrying the colors across the back of the work. You do not have to wind all the yarn you think you might need for the entire knitted article onto the bobbins. Wind just enough yarn on the bobbins so that they are not too heavy or uncomfortable to handle.

To attach the bobbins to your knitting, just tie the yarn from the bobbin over and around the yard you are working with, making a single knot.

To change colors when working an argyle pattern so as to avoid holes, intertwine as just described under Geometric or Abstract Designs.

Jacquard Knitting

The method of changing colors in jacquard knitting depends on the pattern you are following. In some patterns, you can use stranding, but it would be a waste of good yarn to do this for a whole garment if you are able to use one of the other methods. In most designs where a number of colors are used, bobbins are probably the best choice. Where 2 colors are used in a design of more than 4 stitches, weaving is probably the best method to use. And, if there are only 3 stitches between the changes of color in the jacquard design, just carry the color loosely across the back.

Correcting Mistakes

See DROPPED STITCHES; RIPPING OUT

Cowl Neck

Work as described for the crew neck under SWEATERS for about ¾ inch but use

Sweater with cowl neck

a smaller needle. (Using a smaller needle keeps the base of the cowl close to the body.) Change to a larger needle. Then, depending on how full you want the cowl to be, increase stitches evenly across the row. As an example, if you have 60 stitches around the neck and you want the cowl to be fuller than a flat turtleneck, increase by about the number of stitches equal to 2 to 3 inches. With a gauge of 4 stitches to the inch, this means increasing 8 to 12 stitches evenly across the row. Work until the cowl is as deep as you want it to be: If you want a

fuller cowl neck with more of a drop, work half the length you planned, change to the next size larger needle, and work the remainder of length on this needle.

Crochet Hooks

See under EQUIPMENT

Decreasing

Decreasing is working stitches together to eliminate a number of stitches in a row in order to shape a part of the garment or work a pattern stitch.

The simplest direction given in instructions is to decrease one stitch each end of every knit row for so many times. If you have followed such instructions and have done both of the increases the same way, you might have wondered why both edges of the knitted piece do not look the same. Try doing the decreasing this way: Slip the first stitch (in the direction you would knit it) to the right-hand needle. Knit the next stitch. With the left-hand needle, pass the slip stitch over the knit stitch. Knit across the row to the last 2 stitches on the needle. Knit these 2 stitches together. Purl back

the next row. Repeat this, and you will see neatly shaped edges that match.

When knitting any part of a garment that requires shaping on both sides, such

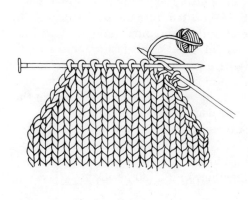

Decreasing at the beginning of a row

Decreasing at the end of a row

as a sleeve or armhole, do the decreasing this same way.

Decreasing is generally done on the knit side because most garments are knitted to be worn on the knit side. If you are knitting a style to be worn on the purl side, do your decreasing on the purl side, as follows: Slip one stitch as if you were purling, purl the next stitch, pass the slip stitch over the purl stitch. At the end of the row, purl 2 stitches together.

If you want a full-fashioned look (where decreases are not made at the edge to be hidden in the seams but are made to be obvious for detail) make the same decreases, but make them two stitches in from the edges: Knit 2, slip 1, knit 1, pass slip stitch over knit stitch; knit to the last 4 stitches; knit 2 stitches together, knit 2; purl back.

Decreasing Evenly Across a Row

When instructions call for decreasing a certain number of stitches in one row, these decreases are usually to be made evenly spaced across the row. To figure out how to do this, divide the number of stitches you have by the number to be decreased. This will tell you where the decreases go. For example, assume you need to decrease 8 stitches in one row and you have 90 stitches in that row. Dividing 90 by 8 gives 11 plus a few stitches, so the decreases are placed 11 stitches apart. Since decreasing involves 2 stitches, you start the decrease 2 stitches before the eleventh stitch, or after you have knitted 9 stitches. So, for each 11 stitches, knit 9, then knit 2 together. This decreases the 11 stitches to 10. Repeat across the row 8 times, and you will have decreased 8 stitches evenly across.

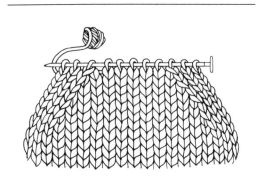

Full-fashioned decreasing

Decreasing on Either Side of a Marker

The stitches decreased on either side of a marker should be decreased in such a way that they slant toward the marker, making an inverted V shape, or away from the marker, making a V shape. For a skirt you probably would want the stitches to slant toward the marker. To accomplish this, knit 1 stitch, pass the slip stitch over the knit stitch *before* the marker, and knit 2 stitches together *after* the marker. Decreases in a raglan sleeve usually slant away from each other. To make this V-shape decrease, knit 2 stitches together *before* the marker; *after* the marker, slip 1 stitch, knit 1 stitch, and pass the slip stitch over the knit stitch.

Decreasing in a Pattern Stitch

If a decrease is required in a pattern stitch, somewhere else in the pattern there is a corresponding increase. This increase can be a yarn-over stitch or any other stitch or method of adding a stitch. This kind of decreasing is not decreasing to shape. It is, rather, a combination of decreasing and increasing to create a pattern or design. Follow the procedure given in the instructions for the pattern so that the decrease slants in the direction intended.

Decreasing on either side of a marker with stitches slanting toward each other

Decreasing on either side of a marker with stitches slanting away from each other

Double Knitting

You can knit stitches that are of double thickness. Such stitches can be used to make a heavy jacket or coat without using bulky yarn. Here are directions for two double-knitted stitches.

METHOD 1: To make a gauge, cast on an even number of stitches. Purl back. For the next row, knit the first stitch, *knit 1 stitch, bring yarn forward as if to purl, slip 1 as if you were going to purl, bring yarn back*. Repeat the instructions between asterisks across the row.

Repeat these two rows for the sample swatch until you have knitted about 5 inches. Knit the next row. Cast off. Measure the swatch across to see how many stitches there are to the inch. Multiply the number of stitches to the inch by the number of inches you need for the width of the garment. *Note:* It is important to note that this type of stitch does not have the same kind of stretch that a simple stockinette stitch has. Therefore, you cannot count on stretching or blocking to size. Instead, allow a little more room by figuring an additional inch or two to the garment.

METHOD 2: This stitch is sometimes called the basket-weave stitch. Start again by working a swatch for gauge. Cast on an even number of stitches. Purl back the first row. For the next row, knit the first stitch, *pass the right-hand needle behind the next stitch on left-hand needle, knit the following stitch from back and leave it on the needle, knit the skipped stitch the regular way and take these 2 stitches off the needles*. Repeat between asterisks across row, ending knit 1. For the second row, purl the second stitch first, leave the original stitch on the needle, purl the first*. Repeat between asterisks across row. Repeat these last two rows for pattern.

Dresses

One-piece Dress

A one-piece dress can be made a number of ways. One-piece dresses with knitted-in waistbands hold more securely and fall better against the hip. However, deciding between a tubular dress or one fitted at the waist is a matter of style and personal taste.

Straight-line Dress with No Waistband
One way to make a straight-line one-piece dress is to take a pullover pattern you like and elongate it. Decide what kind of a hem you want (see HEMS). If the hem you pick is one that is added on after you have finished knitting the dress and serves as a border, decide how many inches this hem border will take up and subtract these inches from the length of the dress to be knitted. Also subtract 1 inch from the length you desire if you are using wool or other natural yarns. This allows for stretching in blocking. For walking room, add 8 inches to the hip measurement to calculate the bottom width at the hem. For example, if your gauge is 4 stitches to the inch, cast on 32 more stitches than the number of stitches given for the cast-on row of the pullover; you will lose these stitches by decreasing at even intervals to the hip (see Straight Skirt, under SKIRTS, for directions on how to make these decreases). For the top of the dress, follow your pullover sweater instructions, working straight until the desired length to the underarm.

Straight-line Dress with Waistline Band   You can make a one-piece dress by making one of the skirts as described under SKIRTS.

After completing the waistband on the skirt and sewing it down into place, take circular needles and pick up a stitch in the front part of each purl stitch at the top of the band. To show you how to complete this dress, we'll work with a gauge of 4 stitches to the inch and with a bust measurement of 34 inches.

FITTED TOP: For a fitted top, place one marker at the beginning of the row and another marker at the halfway point of the row. Then add 1 stitch on either side of the marker every ¾ inch 6 times. This adds the necessary stitches (24) from the waist gradually to the bust, assuming a waist measurement of 28 inches (112 stitches) and a bust measurement of 34 inches (136 stitches). If your size and gauge do not match this example, make a gauge with the yarn you are using (see GAUGE). Multiply the number of stitches to the inch in your gauge by the number of inches needed at the bust. Subtract the number of stitches you have picked up from the waistband. Dividing this number by 4 gives you the number of increases you need to make. Make these increases gradually between the waist and armhole.

Work ½ inch from the last increase and shape the armhole. Work the style of your choice for the rest of the dress, following a printed pattern you like, or make your own instructions by referring to the SWEATERS section of this book.

LOOSE TOP: For a blouson top, using a circular needle, pick up a stitch in each of the purl stitches at the top of the waistband of the finished skirt. In mak-ing a blouson top, the increasing from the waist to the bust is done all in one row, rather than by gradually adding stitches along the sides. Using the same measurements as given in the example for the fitted top and using the same gauge of 4 stitches to the inch, increase the 24 stitches in one row by making 1 increase in every fifth stitch. Work 11 inches to the underarm and continue knitting in the style you wish for the rest of the dress.

Two-piece Dress

Choose a skirt from the section on SKIRTS and make a top to go with it. Read the SWEATERS section for suggestions. If you want a top with no ribbing, to lie flat against the skirt, take the measurement around the body where you want the bottom of the blouse to fall. This measurement is usually about 4 inches more than your waist measurement. Multiply this number of extra inches by the number of stitches to the inch in your gauge. Using a gauge of 4 stitches to the inch, you would cast on 16 stitches more than if you were starting a top with ribbing.

FITTED TOP: If you want the top to be a sweater with ribbing at the bottom, cast on the number of stitches needed for your bust measurement onto a needle two sizes smaller than you are using for the body of the sweater. Work the ribbing and change to the needle you are planning to use for the body of the sweater. Work to the underarm for the length you want and knit the armhole, neckline, sleeve, etc. for the type of top you want.

LOOSE TOP: If you want a loose top,

place markers at the halfway points. Work a border or a hem if desired (see HEMS). Then decrease one stitch on either side of the markers once every inch for 2 inches. Work straight for 5 inches. Then increase 1 stitch before and after each marker every 2 inches 2 times. Work even until piece is 11½ inches or desired length from beginning. Shape armhole and continue for desired top of garment. WAISTBAND: To complete the waistband on the skirt, and on the one-piece dress with the waistline band, see directions at WAISTBANDS.

Dropped Stitches

Picking Up a Dropped Stitch

It is really simple to fix a dropped stitch, especially if you are working in a stockinette stitch.

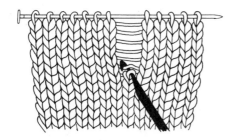

Picking up a dropped stitch

Take a crochet hook and, with the knit side facing you, put the crochet hook into the dropped loop from the front. Extend the hook to reach the last row the stitch dropped from. Hook this yarn with the crochet hook and pull it through the loop. You now have a new loop on your crochet hook. Keeping your crochet hook in this loop, catch the thread on the next row and pull this thread through the loop. Continue doing this until you have picked up all the threads. Place the last loop on the left-hand needle and work.

If you drop a purl stitch while doing ribbing or reverse stockinette, merely turn the article you are knitting, so that the knit side faces you. The purl stitch is a knit stitch on this side. Proceed to pick up the dropped stitch just as you would pick up a knit stitch.

If you drop a stitch while doing a pattern of knit and purl stitches, such as a pattern made of knit 4, purl 4 for 4 rows and then purl 4, knit 4 for 4 rows, turn the garment to the side where the last row dropped is a knit stitch. Pick up the stitches that are knit. When the next stitch you come to is a purl stitch, merely turn the knitted article. Bring the loop to the side facing you and continue picking up each stitch.

If you drop a stitch when working in an intricate design or pattern, it is easier to rip out, rather than try to pick up the dropped stitch. Rip out to the point where the dropped stitch ends. If this is not a knit row, rip down to the next knit row. Pick up the stitches on your needle from the purl side (see RIPPING OUT) so that when all the stitches are picked up, you will be ready to start your work on the knit side of the article.

Dropped Stitches That Create an Openwork Pattern

Perhaps you want to make a lacy stitch but are not ready to attempt a complicated pattern. Lacy stitches can be created by deliberately dropping a stitch in your knitting. But you will have to carefully figure out where you want these dropped stitches to fall. The stitch when dropped cannot be part of an increase or decrease stitch, nor should it be part of a pattern containing any increase or decrease stitches, cables, yarn-overs, or any stitch that combines two or more stitches together. It is best to plan these deliberately dropped stitches for areas of your knitted article that consist simply of knit or purl stitches.

The area of knitting between two separately dropped stitches is called a panel. To determine where to place the dropped stitches in your knitted piece, first decide how many panels you want, not how many dropped stitches. Remember, a back or front of a sweater knitted on straight needles will have one more panel than dropped stitch.

Dropping stitches widens the knitted garment, so when calculating the number of stitches you need for a sweater, subtract 3 inches from your bust measurement. Then take the number of stitches you will have at the bust or chest and divide by the number of stitches in each panel (not dropped stitches) you want. If you are knitting a sweater

on circular needles, you can plan a dropped stitch to fall from the center stitch of the stitches cast off for the armhole. If one of the dropped stitches comes under the arm, when you reach the armhole, drop the stitch and pick up the loop. Put it on the needle and cast off the armhole. If you are making a skirt, plan the panels between the decrease stitches used to shape the skirt.

Vertical Dropped Stitches   Start by determining how far apart you want this lacy stitch to be placed in your knitted piece. As you will see in the following directions for a sample piece, each panel ends with a yarn-over stitch followed by two stitches knitted together. Remember to include these two stitches when figuring for your panels.

In order to make the stitch work, you must start by setting in a base row of yarn-over stitches. These yarn-over stitches serve as a barrier beyond which the stitches will not drop or rip. Here are directions for a sample piece based on 73 stitches, where there are 5 panels of 13 stitches and 4 dropped stitches:

1. Knit 13, place a marker on the right-hand needle, yarn over. You do this by bringing the yarn from behind your work to the front between your two needles. Then place the yarn over your right-hand needle. Keeping this thread on the right-hand needle, knit 2 stitches together. Repeat this across the 73 stitches (K13 yo K2 tog), placing a marker after each K13 stitches.
2. On straight needles, purl back the

next row. Then work back and forth, moving the marker from the left-hand needle to the right-hand needle with each row. When you work on a circular needle, just knit all the time, moving each marker as you come to it.

3. When you are ready to finish off your sample piece, knit to the first marker and move it to the right-hand needle. Drop the next stitch

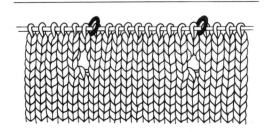

Holes created by yarn-over stitch that forms base of vertical dropped stitch

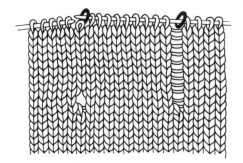

Making the vertical dropped stitch: the dropped stitch near left marker is about to run down to the yarn-over stitch; the dropped stitch at right has already run down.

and run it down. It will stop running at the yarn-over stitch you made on the first row. Repeat this across the row.

Horizontal Dropped Stitches   Here is another way to make an interesting pattern from dropped stitches. In this pattern the dropped stitch goes across the row; that is, it is worked horizontally. These rows with the dropped stitch are separated by rows of stockinette stitch.

1. Work 1 inch in stockinette stitch, finishing by purling the last row if working on straight needles.
2. On the next row: *Knit 1 stitch, yarn over* (done by putting the yarn over the right-hand needle). Repeat between asterisks across the row, ending with knit 1.
3. On the next row: *Purl 1 stitch and drop the yarn over*. Repeat between asterisks across the row. Work straight for 1 inch and repeat.

Horizontal drop stitch

For a longer dropped stitch which will give a more open look to your work, use the following instructions:

ROW 1: *Knit 1, yarn over twice (wrap the yarn around the right-hand needle 2 times)*. Repeat the stitches between the asterisks across the row. End with knit 1.

ROW 2: Work the one stitch, drop the yarn-overs. Repeat across the row.

Drop Shoulder

A drop shoulder is made by working the stitches from the underarm or armhole straight to the shoulder, making no decreases for shaping. Work your sweater or other garment according to your design or instructions up to the armhole. When you reach the point in the front and back of your garment where you would ordinarily cast off stitches at the underarm, do not cast these stitches off. Instead, place a marker at this point and keep knitting even, or straight, making no decreases until you reach the shoulder. Work the shoulder in the usual manner.

The sleeve for a drop shoulder can be made in any way you prefer, full or fitted, up to the cast-off stitches at the armhole. Work the sleeve up to the armhole. To shape, cast off the number of stitches equal to 1 inch at the beginning of the next 4 rows. (For example, if your gauge is 4 stitches to the inch, cast off 4 stitches at the beginning of the next 4 rows.) Then cast off the number of stitches equal to 1½ inches at the beginning of the next 2 rows. (Using the same gauge, this would be 6 stitches.) Cast off the remaining stitches. Weave the seam of the sleeve, and then weave the sleeve into the armhole.

Remember: Even though the top of the sleeve that fits a drop shoulder is shorter than the top of a sleeve that fits a shaped shoulder (such as a set-in sleeve), do not knit the whole sleeve any shorter. The length from underarm to wrist should be the same for all sleeves.

Sweater with drop shoulder

Dry Cleaning

Though I prefer to wash my knitted garments, there are times when dry cleaning is handier and time-saving.

Cleaning, of course, will not keep the garment as fluffy as hand washing.

Check the label on the yarn you've used—is it dry cleanable? Be sure to tell the cleaner what kind of yarn it is. You must emphasize how you want the garment blocked—whether you want it larger or smaller or as is. Some coin-operated cleaning stores, using a good cleaning fluid, can do a batch of sweaters for less money. But you must make sure that the quality of the dry cleaning is good. Try it out by taking an old sweater there first.

Duplicate Stitch

This stitch is used to create a stripe, initials, or any design that can be made of a combination of vertical, horizontal, and diagonal lines. The duplicate stitch covers stitches that have already been knit with stitches of another color. Duplicate stitches can be placed in your knitting in three directions only, forming lines that are vertical, horizontal or diagonal. Use yarn of the same weight as the garment you are applying the duplicate stitch to. When working the duplicate stitch, do not pull the yarn too tightly. The yarn should lie flat on top of the stitch that is being covered. Yarn pulled too tight causes puckering.

Horizontal Duplicate Stitch   Connect yarn at right-hand side where the embroidered line is desired. From the back, place needle at base of the first stitch you want to cover. Pull toward the front. Pass needle under the two loops of the same stitch, going from right to left. Pull through. Go back into base of same stitch from front to back. Place needle into base of next stitch from the back, and repeat for as many stitches as desired.

Vertical Duplicate Stitch   Start at the lowest point. Working from the back, bring needle to the front at the base of the bottom stitch of the stripe. *Place needle under the two loops of the same stitch, going from right to left. Pull through. Put needle into base of stitch, going from front toward the back. Bring needle out in base of stitch directly above, going from back to front, and repeat from asterisk.

Horizontal and vertical duplicate stitches

Diagonal Duplicate Stitch   Start at top of garment and work down. If you work a diagonal from the bottom up you must pull the yarn upward at an angle to get to the next stitch. This prevents the duplicate cover stitch from lying properly.

DIAGONAL SLANTING UPWARD: Start at base of the stitch you want to cover at the bottom of the garment at the right end, at the back. Pull yarn toward the front. Pull needle under the two loops of the same stitch, going from right to left. Pull yarn back into base of same stitch, going from front to back.

Now go into base of stitch one row up and one stitch over to the left. Pull through from back to front; pass needle under the two loops of the same stitch; pull yarn through base of stitch, going from front to back. Continue going one row below and one stitch over until you have completed your diagonal.

DIAGONAL SLANTING DOWNWARD: Starting with the topmost stitch for the diagonal, work exactly as for right diagonal, except that the next stitch you cover will be one row down and one stitch to the left.

Duplicate stitch slanting upward

Duplicate stitch slanting downward

Edges

See FINISHING; BORDER (under CARDIGAN)

Elastic

A thin threadlike elastic can be knitted with your yarn. This is done the same way you weave a second color into the main color you are working with. Hold the elastic thread behind the stitches you are working; when putting the right-hand needle through the stitch on the left-hand needle, go underneath the elastic thread at the same time but do not pull it through the stitch. It will be held in place by the yarn as you knit.

For information about the proper elastic to use in waistbands and for instructions on how to insert it, see WAISTBANDS.

English Knitting Terms

Knitting terms in England sometimes differ from those used in America. Here are the English equivalents of some common American terms.

American	English
stockinette stitch (st st)	stocking stitch (st st)
yarn over (needle) (yo)	wool around (needle) (wrn)
pick up dropped stitch	pick up loops
pick up stitches	knit up stitches
increase (inc)	make a stitch (M1)
skip a stitch	miss a stitch

Equipment

The following knitting aids are usually available in yarn shops and wherever knitting supplies are sold. For many of these knitting aids I have also included tips on how to make your own out of readily available materials, so that you can improvise when necessary. You may not be familiar with some of these aids. Try them. They are very useful.

For information about knitting needles, both straight and circular, see NEEDLES. Make sure to read the discussion of circular needles to find out about new uses for these needles.

Bank Pins

Bank pins are straight pins that are heavy and long. You can buy them at many notions stores. Use them to hold your garment together when sewing seams. These big pins will not fall out or get lost in the yarn.

Bobbins

Bobbins are used when knitting with two or more colors, as in argyle, Aran, or jacquard patterns. They are often made of plastic and can be purchased in yarn stores or notions departments of general stores.

The bobbin will hold the different colors in place and allow you to follow your pattern. Bobbins save you the trouble of carrying strands of yarn across the back of the garment in order to create the pattern. See Argyle Designs in the COLORS section for a discussion of how to attach bobbins to your work.

If you decide to do a pattern requiring bobbins and do not have bobbins on hand, take a piece of cardboard about 2 inches square, make a ¼-inch slit at each end at a slight angle, and wind your yarn around the cardboard in the slits.

Cable-stitch Needles

Cable-stitch needles, or cable holders, are used to slip stitches from your knitting off the regular needle, to be held either in front or in back of the item you are working on until the stitches are needed to complete the cable twist. These stitches are then knitted off the cable holder onto one of the original needles. Cable needles always have points at both ends. They usually come in 7- or 10-inch lengths in all needle sizes and are made of plastic or aluminum. They are available in a variety of shapes. You can use one of a set of double-pointed needles as a substitute for a cable needle. But you also can substitute anything double-pointed that will hold stitches, such as a clean lollipop stick, an opened bobby pin or paper clip, a toothpick, or a crochet hook.

Crochet Hooks

Crochet hooks are needles 5 to 6 inches long with a hook at one end. They are available in steel, aluminum, plastic, or wood. There might still be a few beautiful bone crochet hooks around. If you have one, treasure it.

Steel crochet hooks usually are used for finer work: doilies, bedspreads, and mats. They come in sizes 00 to 14. These

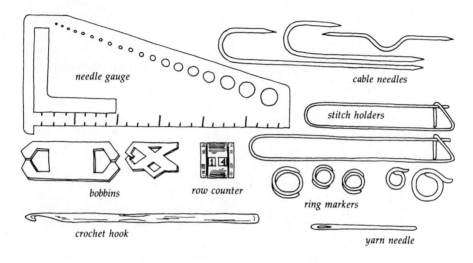

needle gauge

cable needles

stitch holders

bobbins   row counter

ring markers

crochet hook

yarn needle

Equipment

needles are sized so that the higher the number, the finer the needle; the lower the number, the heavier the needle; that is, number 14 is extremely fine and 00 is heavy.

Aluminum and plastic crochet hooks are sold in both numbers and letters (see equivalents table). They are available in sizes A to S, A being the smallest and S the largest.

Crochet hooks are used in knitting to finish off ends, crochet a finish on hems, fronts, or edges, make mesh or picot edges, or pick up dropped stitches.

It is advisable to have at least one hook in each of three sizes. Sizes E, G, and I are the most versatile. With one of

Equivalent Crochet Hook Sizes

American	English
K	2
J	3
I	4
H	5
G	6
F	7
E	8
D	9
C	10
B	11
A	12

these you can usually finish off whatever you are making without having to run to the store at the last minute.

Emery Board

Keep an emery board in your knitting bag. If your nail breaks or if it has a rough spot, file it with the emery board so that it won't catch on the wool as you knit.

Needle Gauge

A needle gauge is used to measure the size (diameter, not length) of a needle. It is made of plastic or metal, with punched holes or slots cut to standard needle sizes. When inserted in the correct place in the gauge, the needle will just fit its own size.

Size markings stamped on the top of needles sometimes wear off, and circular and double-pointed needles never have their sizes printed on them. It is advisable to have a gauge to accurately measure size. You can purchase one at department, notions, or yarn stores.

Ring Markers

These are small colored rings, usually made of plastic. There are two types: rings with a small break and ones that look like tiny coils, that can easily be inserted in the knitting any place on the needle. They are used to separate sections of work or to show where increases or decreases are needed. The marker is always moved from the left-hand needle to the right-hand needle without involving the yarn.

If you have no markers on hand, you can tie a different color yarn on the needle in place of a marker and use it in the same manner. You can also make your own plastic markers from the price tags from bread packages by cutting off some of the tag so that you are left with a circle.

Markers are important. Don't try to make do without them. Guessing where increases and decreases go or where sections begin can be hazardous.

Row Counters

Row counters are used when a pattern varies from row to row or when instructions call for knitting a set number of rows instead of working by inches. They are available in various designs and are made to fit on the back end of straight needles. They cannot be used with circular or double-pointed needles.

Row counters have a dial with consecutive numbers. You turn to the next number every time you finish a row. Turn to the next number *after* finishing a row because you are more apt to remember whether or not you have done so at the end of a row.

You can make your own row counter by punching a hole with your knitting needle in a piece of paper every time you finish a row. This improvised counter works for both straight and circular needles.

Ruler or Tape Measure

It is important that you keep a ruler or tape measure with your knitting to measure lengths and widths accurately. Either fabric tape measures or the roll-up metal type can be used. Make sure your fabric tape measure is plastic coated. Plain fabric tapes react to the weather and shrink or stretch. Today you can purchase tape measures or rulers with metric measures as well as the measures we are used to; such tapes and rulers can be used for knitting instructions from England and other countries on the metric system. We might as well get used to the metric measurements anyway. Everything will be metric soon.

For measuring up to 6 inches you can use a knitting gauge. They are marked with indentations every 2 inches. Knitting gauges have a slide that moves up and down in the middle of the ruler. This slide is particularly useful when you are measuring for the placement of buttonholes.

Scissors

For knitting, get the kind you find most convenient to work with. Many knitters like scissors with long fine points, particularly when seams have to be ripped, but use the scissors you prefer.

Stitch Holders

Stitch holders are like safety pins without the looped end. They come in various lengths from 2 inches up to 10 inches. Usually made of aluminum, they are used to hold stitches that are to be worked later. If none is available when you need one, you can make your own stitch holder by pulling a length of yarn through the stitches to be held, with a tapestry needle or crochet hook, and tying the ends of the yarn together. This will hold as well as any stitch holder. Do not use safety pins as substitutes for stitch holders. The stitches get caught in the looped ends of the safety pin and may break.

Yarn Needles

These are large-eyed needles, usually in steel or plastic, with a blunt point used for sewing seams, weaving two pieces together, or darning. They look like a sewing needle but have a larger eye and are thicker. They come in various sizes and lengths. The two sizes that are most convenient to have on hand are a medium-size and large-size needle. These will work for most yarns.

Yarn needles are also called *darning needles* and *tapestry needles*. Do not buy small needles intended for needlepoint, since the eye of a needlepoint needle is usually too small for most knitting yarns.

Errors

See DROPPED STITCHES; RIPPING OUT

Facings

A facing allows a sweater, jacket, or coat front to be folded back and still show a finished surface. Here are some different types of facings.

Even Facing with No Lapel

This facing starts at the bottom of the garment and is knit in one piece with it. Decide on how wide you want the facing to be. Multiply this dimension by the number of stitches to the inch of the yarn you are using. Add this number of stitches plus 1 to both fronts of the garment. The extra stitch is for a slip stitch where the facing folds back.

For example, you are getting 7 stitches to 2 inches when you work your gauge swatch, and you decide that you want a 2-inch facing. For the right front, cast on 7 stitches for the facing plus 1 stitch for

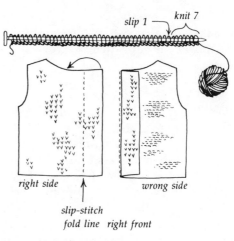

Facing with no lapel

the fold-back and then cast on the number of stitches you need for the right front. Purl back row. Work as follows:

ROW 1: Knit 7, slip 1, knit the rest of the row (or work it in your pattern stitch).

ROW 2: Purl back (or work your pattern stitch), purling the last 8 stitches.

On the left front, cast on the 7 stitches plus the 1 fold-back stitch at the end of the row after you have cast on the stitches needed for the left front. Purl back. Work as follows:

ROW 1: Knit the stitches for the left front up to the last 8 stitches. Slip 1 stitch and knit the last 7 stitches.

ROW 2: Purl the first 8 stitches and work the rest of the row following the pattern stitch for the left front.

Make sure always to make the slip stitch over the slip stitch two rows below.

Facing with Lapel

Work this facing the same as the Even Facing just described, up to 1 inch below the shaping for the armhole. Then increase 1 stitch at the beginning of the right front (or at the end on the left front) of every knit row up to the neck. This facing can be turned back as a lapel.

Make sure to continue the slip stitch on every knit row over the slip stitch two rows below.

Extended Facing

This facing extends into the outer edge of the garment. Let us again assume that you want a 2-inch facing and that your

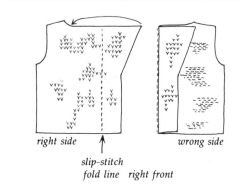

right side   *wrong side*

slip-stitch
fold line   right front

Facing with lapel

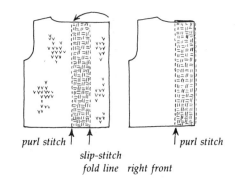

purl stitch   *purl stitch*

slip-stitch
fold line   right front

Extended facing

gauge is 7 stitches to 2 inches. For the right front, cast on 7 stitches plus 1 stitch upon which the facing will be folded and then cast on the number of stitches needed for the right front. Work as follows:

ROW 1: Knit 7 stitches, slip 1 (for the fold-back stitch), knit 7, purl

1, knit the rest of the stitches for the right front.

ROW 2: Work the stitches for the right front up to the last 15 stitches. Knit the stitch you purled on Row 1 and purl the rest of the stitches.

Work the facing straight up as described under Even Facing or increase for a lapel as described under Facing with Lapel. Make sure you continue the slip stitch on every knit row over the slip stitch two rows below.

You can, if you choose, work the stitch in the panel created between the slip stitch and the purl stitch in the pattern stitch as the rest of your garment, or you can use a different pattern stitch in this panel. Work other front to correspond.
Finishing the Facing Turn back the facing on both fronts, folding on the slip stitch. Sew the lapels into place.

the yarn where the sides of the garment will fall.

2. When casting off the shoulder, make sure you cast off from the outer armhole toward the neck. When you break the yarn, make sure you leave a piece of yarn long enough to weave the shoulders together.

3. When starting a sleeve, make sure you leave a long end that can later be used to sew up the sleeve seam.

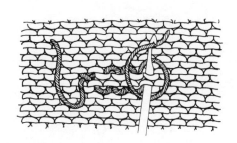

Cleaning up ends

Finishing

Cleaning Up Ends

If you make proper use of your yarn while knitting, you will find that you have to do very little finishing of end pieces of yarn. Here are three good ways to cut down on the number of ends:

1. Always try to connect a new piece of yarn at the beginning of a row. Then you can use it to sew the seam. If you are working on a circular needle, connect

To clean up the ends when you have finished knitting and sewing the garment together, turn the garment inside out. Make sure all the ends are pulled through to the wrong side. Then, with a crochet hook or yarn needle, turn the yarn into a circle following the direction of the next stitch. Go into the stitch, come out in front of the curve, and pull the yarn through. Follow the next 2 stitches in the same way. Push the end under the next stitch. Before cutting the end of the yarn, stretch the knitted piece with your hands to allow the end to settle into place. Then cut.

When finishing ends along a seam, follow the same procedure going along the seam.

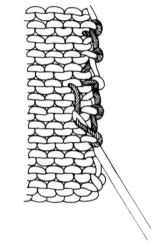

Cleaning up yarn at seam

When cleaning up ends of yarn for a garment made of more than one color, be sure to work the end of each color into stitches or seams of the same color wherever possible.

Edges

Edges of Front-opening Garment   If you do not finish the front edges of a

sweater, coat, or other garment that opens down the front, you will find that the lower part of the front will tend to fall toward the back when the garment is worn and that front edges will not lie flat. In order to prevent this, you need to add a row of stitches to control the front edge. The best way to do this is to work a row of crocheted slip stitches along the edges.

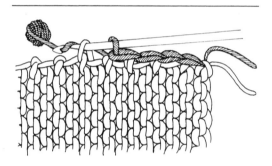

Finishing edge of front-opening garment with slip stitch

Pick up the garment, keeping the wrong side facing you. Connect the yarn in the right-hand corner stitch. You have knitted the first stitch in each row and worked it again on the row back. This produces a nub at the end of every other row. With a crochet hook one size larger than you would use if you were to crochet with the yarn used in the garment, work a slip stitch through each nub along the edge. You use a hook one size larger when making a slip stitch to keep you from working the slip stitch too tightly. You want the stitch to lie flat along the edge—not to draw in or stretch the edge (see SLIP STITCHES).

Check to make sure that the edge is flat and that the slip stitches have not pulled the edges up so that the fronts of the garment are no longer even at the bottom. If the slip stitch is too tight, rip it out and do it more loosely.

You might have the reverse problem. There may be so many slip stitches at the edge that the edge will appear rippled. If this happens, rip out the slip stitches and start again, skipping some nubs along the front edges as you put in the new stitches, or placing the hook into two successive nubs before taking the yarn over the hook and slipping the stitch.

For a knitted edge see Borders under CARDIGANS.

side facing you and the edge you want to finish at the top. Connect the yarn with a crochet hook, using the same size hook you would use if you were knitting the yarn.

Crochet stitches usually work larger than knit stitches. To keep the edge flat, it is necessary to skip them occasionally. Start by working a slip stitch (see SLIP STITCHES) in each edge stitch. Skip 1 stitch about every 2 inches. Or, instead of skipping the stitch, you can put the crochet hook into the front of each of two stitches, pulling a loop through both stitches.

Keeping an edge flat by making 1 slip stitch in 2 edge stitches

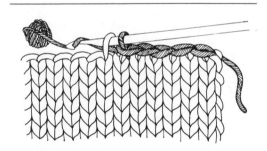

Finishing edge by making a slip stitch in every stitch

Edge at Bottom of Garment or Around Neck Hold the garment with the right

To make sure you are keeping the edge flat, lay the garment on a flat surface. If there is no ripple, everything is OK. If there is a slight ripple, you are working your crochet stitch too loosely, or you will have to skip a stitch a little more often. When you reach the end of the row, turn the garment and, with the wrong side facing you, do a row of single crochet, working a single-crochet stitch in each slip stitch.

If you want to lengthen the skirt or add to the neckline edge, you can continue working in this manner for the desired length.

Here is a way to make this edge using knit stitches instead of crocheting. With the right side of the work facing you, pick up stitches along the edge, using the same needle you used for the garment. If you are picking up stitches on a purl-stitch turning row, such as you might have at the bottom of a skirt, pick up the front of each purl stitch only for the edge stitches. Turn and cast off loosely on the wrong side, using a purl stitch when casting off.

Flat Knitting

This method of knitting can only be used for garments that are worked on straight needles. It can not be used on garments made in the round, such as skirts.

Knit the first row. When you have finished the first row, do not turn the knitting to the purl side as you usually do. Just knit back with the left hand, going from left to right to the beginning of the row.

Fringe

Cut a piece of cardboard 1 inch longer than the length of the fringe you want. Decide how many strands you want in the fringe; the more strands, the thicker. Decide on the style of fringe you want—single fringe in every stitch or groups of fringe regularly spaced. Remember that when you make the fringe, each strand will be folded in half. Therefore, if you wish a 4-strand fringe, you will need only 2 strands of yarn for each fringe. If you decide on a 6-strand fringe, you will need 3 strands of yarn.

Spaced Fringe

If you plan to space the fringe along the edge, first figure out how much you need. To do this, take the knitted article and mark each corner or seam. You certainly want fringe there. Fold the article in half. Mark the center point. Fold this half in half and again mark for fringe at the fold. Continue folding and marking the space between fringes until the fringes are as close as you want them to be. Remember, if you place fringes of more than 2 strands too close, you will get a ripple effect, and if you place them too far apart, they will look straggly.

Now you know how many fringes you need. Multiply this by the number of strands you want in each fringe. Wind uncut yarn around the cardboard you have cut as many times as equals your total number of strands. If all this yarn will not fit on the cardboard, cut it in batches. Remember that a 6-strand fringe requires only 3 strands of yarn. So, for a

6-strand fringe, wind your yarn 3 times around the cardboard. Break the yarn.

Spaced fringe

With scissors, cut the yarn along one edge of the cardboard. Take the number of strands you need for the fringe. Fold the strands in half. Take a crochet hook. Keeping the right side of the knitted article facing you, put the crochet hook into the article from the underside to the right side at one of the places you marked for the fringe. With the hook of the crochet needle, catch the loop made by the folded strands and pull it through to the back of the article. Then, with the crochet hook, catch all strands of the fringe. Making sure that the ends of the fringe are even, pull the strands through the loop and flatten them. Repeat until all the fringes are attached.

Double Fringe

After doing this you can create a more elaborate fringe. Here is how to make a double fringe. Take half the strands from the first fringe and half the strands from the second fringe and hold them together. Place your fingers at the point you want the second joining of the fringes. Bring all the strands over toward the right, then up and back down through the loop formed at finger point. Pull the ends of the fringe into place.

Double fringe

Knitted Loop Fringe

Decide how dense a looped fringe will look best on your knitted garment. You can make a very close looping, if you make your knitted loops every other row, that will give your knitted piece a ruglike look. If you prefer a striped effect, make the loops every fourth row. Or you can make a wide border of loops by repeating the loop row as many times as you wish at the bottom of the garment.

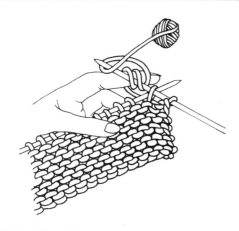

Knitted loop fringe

Knitted loop fringe is best done on the purl side. Always work the first stitch plain; that is, without any loops. Wrap the yarn around your forefinger twice, wrapping toward you. Place the right-hand needle into the front of the next stitch on your needle and then into the loops on your finger. Then wrap the yarn around the needle and pull it through the two loops and the stitch on the needle to make one stitch. Purl the next stitch. Repeat this procedure across

the row, making the last stitch a plain stitch. Use a spare needle or a pencil to pull the loops even. For larger loops, just wind the yarn around the forefinger and the needle more loosely. After you have completed the row of loops, on the next row knit the groups of stitches in each loop as one stitch.

Fur Knitting

Before undertaking a project with fur, work up a piece large enough so you can see how the fur you have chosen is going to react. Make sure that the fur you choose has been stretched before you begin to cut it. Check with a furrier if you are not sure of the fur you have bought. Also find out if the garment you are planning will stretch when blocked when it is finished. Take this stretch into account in planning your garment.

Begin by cutting the fur into strips about ¼ to ⅜ inch wide. Overlap the short ends and stitch them together firmly to make long strips. Fur works very well when knitted with wool, and for your first project I recommend working the fur with wool.

Try different-size needles to find the needle that gives the closeness necessary for a firm garment. When knitting the fur, place the fur over the needle with the pelt side up so that the stitch will come up with the fur facing you. An easy pattern to try is one in which you knit two rows of yarn followed by two rows of fur. Work up a swatch about 6 inches square in this pattern.

Your first attempt in working with fur should be the simplest jacket or coat you can make. A box or unfitted coat or jacket would be the best. When figuring out the measurements for your jacket or coat, allow for the fact that you will probably be wearing a bulky sweater or a jacket underneath. Do not plan to knit a tightly fitting coat or jacket. Make the armholes deeper than you usually would. The dimension across the back, measured about 3 inches below the shoulder, should be at least 3 inches wider than your measurement at this point, and the shoulder should be at least 1 inch wider than you would ordi-narily knit a shoulder. Make each front at least 3 inches wider than half the back to allow for the overlap of the coat or jacket in the front closing. Remember to subtract the number of inches that you can stretch the length of the sleeve from the sleeve dimensions.

When sewing the seams together, use a matching wool folded double or use 2 strands and weave seams together.

Finishing the edges all the way around should be done in yarn only in a crochet slip stitch, after the garment is blocked, working the slip stitches so that they have enough give and do not pull in the edges of the garment. You do not want the finishing stitches to draw up along the front or draw in along the bottom.

Gauge

Most people look at the gauge given in instructions and assume that, if they use the yarn and the needles recommended, the garment they are making will automatically come out correct. Not so.

The needle size given in instructions is the one used by the person who made the garment when knitting with the recommended yarn. That person using that yarn and those needles got the gauge given. You, on the other hand, using the same yarn and the same size needles and following the same instructions, may produce a garment that comes out either larger or smaller. The instructions are not necessarily wrong. The problem is the gauge. A gauge is always provided for your guidance, and your gauge must match the one given in the instructions for your garment to come out right.

To check if your gauge is the same, the first thing you must do before knitting the garment is to knit a sample swatch. Take the yarn and the needles called for and cast on 20 stitches. Work about 4 inches in the stitch specified in the instructions. Take this piece *off* the needle and pin it down on something firm. Be careful not to stretch it.

Stitches per Inch   Place a tape measure across the swatch so that the beginning of the tape is between two stitches. Measure 2 inches across. Put a pin in the last stitch corresponding to the 2-inch mark on the tape. Count the number of stitches between the beginning of the tape and the 2-inch pin mark.

Let us say that the gauge in the instructions is 4 stitches to the inch. When you measure your piece of knitting, you find you get 9 stitches to 2 inches (4½ stitches to the inch). "Not so

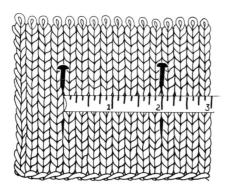

Measuring stitches per inch: the gauge of this sample is 4 stitches to the inch

bad," you say. "It's close enough." Let's see if that is true. Your instructions call for 126 stitches. Dividing 126 stitches by 4 (the number of stitches in the gauge per inch), you get 31½ inches. Dividing 126 stitches by your 4½ stitches—you get 28 inches. Your sweater will come out 3½ inches too narrow.

Now let's assume when you measure your piece of knitting you get 7 stitches to 2 inches (3½ stitches to the inch). Dividing 126 stitches by 3½ stitches, you get 36 inches—4½ inches too large.

How to solve this? Let's take the first example, where you get 9 stitches to 2 inches, or 4½ stitches to the inch. In this case, use a needle one size *larger* to get fewer stitches to the inch. Make another swatch and see if you get the correct gauge. If it still is not correct, either try a

needle another size larger or work a little looser.

In the second example, where you get too few stitches to the inch, use a needle one size smaller. Work up a new swatch. This should give you the correct gauge. If it doesn't, try a needle another size smaller or work a little tighter.

Hint: A garment made slightly on the smaller side is fine if made of natural yarns. These yarns have a natural elasticity, so it is very simple to block to size 1 or 2 inches wider or longer.

I usually prefer not to block the swatch used for gauge. It's best to make your adjustments by blocking after the garment is finished.

Rows per Inch To measure rows to the inch, lay your tape measure along the outside of a row of stitches down the middle of the sample swatch. Do not lay the tape measure along the outer edge. Make sure that the tape is straight along the stitches' edges for at least 2 inches. Place a pin at right angles to the tape at the top of the tape. Place another pin at right angles to the tape at a point 2 inches below. Count the number of rows between the pins and divide by 2 for the number of rows to the inch.

If the number of rows to the inch that you measure in this sample swatch is not the same as called for in your instructions, follow the number of *inches* called for in your instructions for length, not the number of rows. If rows are given in the instructions, translate this into inches. For example, the gauge in the instructions is 5 rows to the inch and you are getting 6 rows in your gauge.

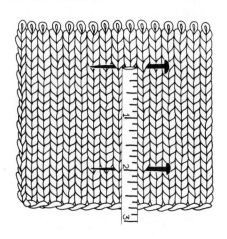

Measuring rows per inch: there are 6 rows per inch in this sample

You come to a place in your instructions that says work 15 rows. According to the gauge given, this equals 3 inches. So work 3 inches, or 18 rows in your gauge.

If the garment you are making has a pattern that requires a certain number of rows and your gauge does not match that of the instructions, make the garment a bit shorter or longer so that you knit the correct number of rows for the pattern to come out properly.

Geometric or Abstract Designs

See under COLORS, CHANGING

Gloves

Gloves can be made of almost any yarn. Choose wool for winter wear, cotton for summer, and rayon or silk for evening. Gloves are usually made on sets of 4 or 5 double-pointed needles, 4 being preferable. Use needles one or two sizes smaller for the wrist band than for the hand part. If you prefer a firm fit on the fingers, you can go back to the smaller needles when knitting the fingers.

Measure around the palm at the widest part of the hand, without including the thumb. Make up a gauge using the yarn and the size needle you plan to use for the body of the glove (see GAUGE). Multiply the number of stitches per inch (as determined by the gauge swatch) by the measurement around the palm of the hand. This tells you the number of stitches to cast on to start the glove. Measure the hand around the palm again, but this time include the thumb. This measurement determines how many stitches are needed when increasing to make the thumb.

CUFF: Cast on the number of stitches you have determined you need to start the glove. Divide them among 3 needles. Let us assume you are using sport yarn and are getting 5 stitches to the inch. The palm measures 7 inches. Multiplying 7 inches by 5 stitches to the inch gives us 35 stitches. Since 35 is not divided evenly by 3, cast on 36 stitches, placing 12 stitches on each needle. Use the smaller size needles when casting on.

Work in ribbing for the desired length

of the cuff. To make the gloves fit closer at the wrist, change to needles one or two sizes smaller and work 1 inch. Change back to the larger needles and work 2 rows.

RIGHT THUMB: To start the thumb, increase 1 stitch at the beginning of the first needle by picking up the back of the first stitch. Place this stitch on the needle, knit it, and knit all the rest of the stitches around. Work 2 rounds plain; that is, without any increasing. Then repeat the increase, using the same method as before.

Now refer to the measurement that included the thumb. Say it is 8½ inches, 1½ inches more than the palm measurement. This means you need to add stitches until you have increased 1½ inches. With a gauge of 5 stitches to the inch, this means you need to add 7½ stitches, but since you cannot add half a stitch, make it 8 stitches. Now you begin to increase on each side of the thumb: 2 stitches in each increase round 4 times, or a total of 8 increases. Here's how to do this.

Increase at the beginning of the first needle as before. Knit 3. Increase by picking up the back of the third stitch you knitted, place it on the needle, and knit it. Knit all the rest of the stitches in the round, making no more increases. Note that in this round you started with 3 stitches between the increases. Now there are 5 stitches between the increases. Work 1 round plain.

Repeat the increases. This time there are 7 stitches between them. Work 1 round plain. Repeat the increases twice again (first there are 9 stitches between them and then 11 stitches), working every other row plain. You now have 13 stitches for the right thumb.

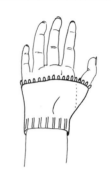

Checking length of thumb

Arrangement of stitches for thumb

The best way to judge whether the thumb is correct (especially the first time you make a glove) is to try the glove on. Check to see if the knitted thumb stretches comfortably around the curve between the thumb and the palm of your hand. Remember that the glove will be pulled down between the thumb and the palm when worn. If this section looks too short or feels too narrow, add one more increase round and one more plain round. If the thumb fits well, proceed to finish it.

Assuming you have increased once more, there are now 15 stitches for the thumb on the needle. Divide these stitches between 2 needles. Cast 5 stitches onto a third needle and join the 20 stitches. Place the remaining stitches on a piece of yarn or on 2 small stitch holders. Work 2 rows around the thumb. Now begin to decrease on the 5-stitch needle. To do this, decrease 1 stitch by knitting 2 together on the needle. Work 1 round plain. Decrease another stitch on the same needle. Work 1 round plain. Decrease 1 stitch on the same needle. Work 1 round plain. Decrease again on this needle.

Now there is only 1 stitch remaining on this needle, but there is a total of 16 stitches on the 3 needles that hold the stitches for the thumb. Divide these among the 3 thumb needles and work straight (that is, without any decreasing) until the knitted thumb is long enough to reach the top of the thumb of the hand (not the top of the nail). Decrease 2 stitches on every row around until 4 stitches remain. Do not make these decreases next to each other, but space them evenly.

Finish by any of the following methods:

METHOD 1: Break the yarn about 5 inches from the end of the thumb. Thread the yarn into a yarn needle and run it through the 4 stitches. Pull the stitches together. Turn glove inside out and finish off the yarn (see FINISHING).

METHOD 2: Turn the glove inside out and overcast the stitches (see Overcasting under SEAMS). If this is not done carefully, the inside of the glove may feel lumpy.

METHOD 3: These stitches can be grafted (see GRAFTING).

HAND: To work the right hand, return to the base of the thumb. Using a free needle, pick up 5 stitches from the stitches that were cast on for the thumb. This will give you a total of 40 stitches for the palm of the glove. Place the stitches you put on the piece of yarn back on the needles and, working around on these stitches, knit until you reach the needle with the 5 stitches you picked up. Increase 1 stitch in the first of these 5 stitches and 1 stitch in the last of these 5 stitches. There are now 42 stitches on 3 needles. Working around, make decreases on the needle that has the 7 stitches as follows: Knit 2 stitches together 2 times on the second row around. Work 1 row with no decreases. Decrease 1 stitch in the center of the same needle every other row until one stitch remains.

Now there is a total of 36 stitches on the needles. Continue working, making no more decreases until the palm measures 1½ inches from the base of the thumb.

Shift the stitches from the other 2 needles to divide stitches more equally. Place a piece of yarn on the single stitch left from the thumb side. Use this as the marker for setting up the forefinger.

Arrangement of stitches for finger

For the *small finger*, take 5 stitches from back of glove and the remaining 4 stitches from the palm. Pick up 3 stitches from the cast-on stitches of ring finger. Work to about ¾ inch less than the ring finger. Finish off.

LEFT-HAND GLOVE: For the left hand, reverse the glove. Be sure that the 4 stitches from the palm are picked up from the right of the marked stitch. Work as right-hand glove.

FINGERS: For the *right-hand index finger*, use 4 stitches from the palm side of the glove, the stitch you marked, and 6 stitches from the back part of the glove. Place the remaining stitches on a piece of yarn. This gives you space to work the finger.

Cast on 3 stitches between the palm and the back of the glove. Now there are 14 stitches for the index finger. Divide these stitches among 3 needles. Work up to the top of the finger (again, trying the glove on is the best way for measuring length). Finish in the same way you finished the thumb.

For the *middle finger*, take the next 4 stitches from back of glove, pick up 2 stitches from the cast-on stitches on first finger, and take 4 stitches from the palm of glove. Cast on 3 stitches between the back and the palm of the glove. Work even for a little longer than you did for the first finger, about 2 rows. Make sure you have the length you want for the finger and then finish off as before.

Repeat for the *ring finger*.

Grafting

Grafting is a method used to connect two edges that are still on the needle. Grafting is the preferred method of finishing the toe of a sock and can be used to finish the fingertips of gloves. It can also be used if you pull and snag a knitted garment and the two sections separate.

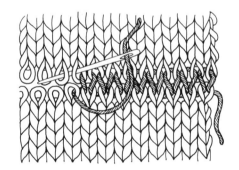

Grafting

Place the two edges to be grafted so they face each other. Using a yarn needle threaded with matching yarn, come from the back of the first stitch of the lower piece toward the front. *Then go into the first stitch of the upper piece from the front of the stitch toward the back. Come up into the next stitch from back to front. Then go back in through the front of the first stitch, going toward the back; then from the back into the next stitch going toward the front.* Repeat between asterisks until all the stitches you want grafted are completed. Bring the yarn to the wrong side of the work and finish off (see Cleaning Up Ends under FINISHING).

Gussets

Gussets are diamond-shaped pieces knitted separately and inserted at the underarms of a coat or jacket. They serve to make the armhole deeper and more comfortable without adding bulk to the sleeve. When making a gusset, you must remember that the area into which you are placing the gusset must be shaped exactly to match it.

Gusset for
Underarm of a Coat or Jacket

A gusset is made starting at the bottom point. Stitches are added by increasing 1 stitch on each end every other row until the width desired is reached, and then the stitches are decreased every other

row until the end point is reached. This creates the diamond shape. To make a gusset:

1. Cast on 2 stitches and purl back.
2. Increase in the first stitch. To make this increase, knit the stitch, pick up the side of the stitch from the row below, and knit it.
3. Increase in the second stitch. To make this increase, pick up the stitch from the side of the stitch of the row below, knit it, and then knit the last stitch.
4. Purl back these 4 stitches. Turn.
5. Increase in the first stitch as just described. Knit 2 stitches. Increase in the last stitch as described.
6. Purl back.

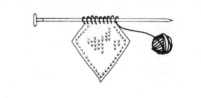

Gusset

Continue in this manner for 2½ inches, measuring from the center of the gusset down to the starting point. Then work 2 rows with no increases. This is the midpoint of the gusset. You now begin decreasing at the beginning and end of every knit row, as follows:

1. To make the first decrease, slip the first stitch, knit the next stitch, and pass the slip stitch over the knit stitch.
2. Knit to the last 2 stitches and knit these together.

Repeat these decreases every knit row until 2 stitches remain. Cast off.

The armhole for the gusset must be shaped the same way. To do this, work the back piece of your garment 2 inches shorter than the measurement your instructions indicate for the armhole decrease. Decrease at the beginning and end of every knit row of the back the same number of times as you did on the gusset. Then work even until the armhole is the desired length to the shoulder.

Follow this procedure at the armhole side of each front, starting the decreases 2 inches before the armhole. Knit the sleeve 2 inches shorter than your instructions indicate is needed to the armhole.

Decrease at the beginning and end of every knit row the same number of times you decreased for the gusset. Then cast off 4 stitches at the beginning of every row for 4 rows. Cast off. Weave the gusset into the coat or jacket.

Gusset inserted into a jacket

Hats

There are hats for all seasons, but most are made to wear in cold weather. They can be made of any yarn. Make sure you make a GAUGE for the yarn you plan to use. When measuring the number of stitches to the inch, put the gauge swatch down on a flat surface and do not stretch it when measuring.

Choose a stitch that has stretch in it, so that the hat will go over the head easily but will fit properly. The give in a knitted hat comes from the stitch as well as the yarn. Synthetics and yarns such as cotton and linen, which have little give, must be worked in a stretchy stitch. Hats made of wool or other natural fibers that have more stretch can be made in a stockinette or other less stretchy stitch. Here are some stretchy stitches particularly suitable for hats, whether made of wool or other yarns.

Knit 2, Purl 2 Rib   Cast on a number of stitches divisible by 4 (multiple of 4).

> Knit 2, purl 2 across the row. Repeat this row for the pattern.

Brioche Rib   This stitch creates a thick rib, but no purl stitches are used. Cast on a number of stitches divisible by 2 (multiple of 2).

> ROW 1: Knit.
> ROW 2: *Knit 1, knit next stitch by knitting into the stitch below the needle*. Repeat the stitches between asterisks up to the last 2 stitches. Knit the last 2 stitches.

Repeat Row 2 for pattern.

Moss Knit Rib   Cast on a number of stitches divisible by 4 (multiple of 4).

> ROW 1: *Knit 3, purl 1*. Repeat across the row.

ROW 2: *Knit 2, purl 1, knit 1*. Repeat across the row.
Repeat these 2 rows for pattern.

Spiral Rib   Cast on a number of stitches divisible by 6 (multiple of 6).

ROWS 1, 2, 3: *Knit 3, purl 3*. Repeat across row.
ROW 4: *Purl 1, knit 3, purl 2*. Repeat across row.
ROW 5: *Knit 2, purl 3, knit 1*. Repeat across row.
ROW 6: Same as Row 4.
ROW 7: *Knit 1, purl 3, knit 2*. Repeat across row.
ROW 8: *Purl 2, knit 3, purl 1*. Repeat across row.
ROW 9: Same as Row 7.
ROWS 10, 11, 12: *Purl 3, knit 3*. Repeat across row.
ROW 13: Same as Row 8.
ROW 14: Same as Row 7.
ROW 15: Same as Row 8.
ROW 16: Same as Row 5.
ROW 17: Same as Row 4.
ROW 18: Same as Row 5.
Repeat these 18 rows for pattern.

Stocking Hat

A basic hat is the stocking hat, also known as a watch cap. Cropped short, it can be a beanie or skull cap. Select the pattern stitch you want to use for this hat and then make a gauge swatch. Multiply the number of stitches to the inch in your gauge by 18 inches, the average width at the bottom of a stocking hat. With knitting-worsted-weight yarn, you should get 7 stitches to 2 inches (3½

stitches to the inch). With bulky yarn, you should get 2½ stitches to the inch.

The preceding patterns are all worked around a multiple of stitches (see Multiple of Stitches under INSTRUCTIONS). In order for these patterns to work properly, the multiple of stitches called for must not be changed. You have calculated the number of stitches you need for the starting row of your hat. If this number is not divisible exactly by the number of stitches in the multiple given in the pattern, cast on the nearest number of stitches that will equal the multiple needed.

Decide if you want a cuff on the hat. Work the pattern evenly, with no decreases or increases, for at least 5½ inches. Work up to 10 inches or longer, if you want to turn back the hat for a cuff. The depth you work depends on how deep you want the cuff.

Change the stitch to a knit 1, purl 1 rib, and knit in this ribbing for 1½ inches. This is the part of the hat that fits over the top of the head. Decrease in the next row as follows: Slip 1 stitch, knit 1 stitch, pass the slip stitch over the knit stitch across the row. Purl back. Then decrease by knitting 2 stitches together across the row; purl back. Repeat the last two rows until 7 to 9 stitches are left on the needle.

Break the yarn about 20 inches from the top of the hat and thread a yarn needle with it. Run the needle through the stitches remaining, starting at the end of the row (from last to first stitch). Pull the stitches together. Then, with the same yarn, continue to weave the side seam of the hat (see WEAVING).

Beret

Cast on 7 stitches. Purl back the next row.

ROW 1: Increase 1 stitch in each of the 7 stitches.
ROW 2: Purl.
ROW 3: *Knit 1 stitch, increase 1 stitch*. Repeat across row.
ROW 4: Purl back; continue purling on all even rows.
ROW 5: *Knit 2 stitches, increase 1 stitch*. Repeat across row.
ROW 7: *Knit 3 stitches, increase 1 stitch*. Repeat across row.
ROW 9: *Knit 4 stitches, increase 1 stitch*. Repeat across row.

Continue increasing in this way, knitting one stitch extra between increases, until the beret measures 11 inches across (5½ inches from center to end) for a small beret, 12½ inches across (6¼ inches from center to end) for a medium beret, 14 inches across (7 inches from center to end) for a large beret. Do *not* measure along the increase line; measure in the center between the increases.

Work 2 rows even. Decrease 10 stitches in the next row, evenly spaced (see Decreasing Evenly Across a Row under DE-CREASING). Disregard the fact that you may have a few extra stitches at the end.

Knit the next 2 rows plain; that is, with no decreases. Decrease by 10 stitches again on the next row. If you had those few extra stitches, you can start your next decrease after you have knitted those extra stitches. Work 2 rows even.

Continue decreasing in this way until you have a beret that fits the head. The best way of determining this is by referring to the sample gauge that you knitted before you started the beret. Take the number of stitches you have to the inch and multiply by 18 inches. This tells you the number of stitches necessary for the beret to fit the head. The decreased section should be 2½ to 3 inches in depth, depending on the kind of beret you like. (Remember, everyone does not like the same beret, with the same width across or with the same depth. You make this the way *you* like it.) Now, if you want the beret to just end here, cast off loosely. I suggest as a finishing stitch a row of SLIP STITCHES made with a crochet hook all around the cast-off stitches.

If you prefer a band, do not cast off, but continue working evenly for 1 inch. If you want to stop here, you can cast off and slip-stitch the edge.

If you prefer a double or folded-over band, work the 1-inch band, as described, and then purl 1 row on the knit side. Knit, working 1 row less than 1 inch. Cast off the stitches, leaving enough yarn to sew the band down. Turn the band to the inside on the purl row. Sew in place. Crochet a slip stitch through the purl stitch at the fold.

Hems

Hems finish off the lower edge of a jacket, sweater, coat, skirt, or sleeve. Hems that are turned back and sewed in place, such as the ones you are familiar with in sewn clothes, are structured hems. They are usually made as part of the garment. Those which are not turned back and sewn are called unstructured hems, or borders. They are usually added to the finished garment. Both types of hems hold the edge flat, keep it in place, and give the garment a finished look.

You can make these hems on the bottoms of garments or sleeves where there is no ribbing. You can substitute these hems for ribbed borders that your instructions call for.

Structured Hems

Decide on the depth of hem you need. Usually a hem is 1 to 1½ inches deep. A structured hem has the same number of stitches as the first row of the garment. To substitute a structured hem in a pattern calling for a ribbed border, use the number of stitches given in the first row above the ribbing as the number of stitches for the first row of your hem. In making such a substitution, remember that garments with ribbed edges are usually styled shorter than those with hemmed edges, so adjust your garment's length accordingly.

ON A CIRCULAR NEEDLE: Join your stitches in a circle, making sure all the stitch bottoms are even before you start to knit. Knit 1 row. Check again to make sure all stitches are straight (see Circular Needles under NEEDLES for illustration).

Knit 1 inch or the depth of the hem chosen. Purl 1 row; this is the hemline or turning line of your hem. Continue, changing to the stitch called for in the pattern for your garment or plain knit if the skirt is made in stockinette stitch.

ON STRAIGHT NEEDLES: Skirts made on straight needles are usually done in two halves. Cast on the number of stitches you need for one half. Work in the stockinette stitch for the depth of the hem you have decided upon, ending with a purl row. Purl the next row for the hemline, or turning row. Purl the next row to bring you back to the right side of your garment. Continue, following your pattern. Make another half to match. Weave the side seams together (see WEAVING for instructions on sewing a flat seam). When finished with your garment, turn back the hem, making the purl row the edge of the garment, and sew the hem in place, using a yarn needle.

As a final finishing, hold the garment with the right side facing you so that the purl row of the hem is on top. Connect the yarn to the beginning of the purl row. With a crochet hook, chain one stitch and work SLIP STITCHES in the front part of the purl stitches formed by the purl row. Work a slip stitch in each purl

Attaching yarn and chaining 1 stitch

stitch to the end of the row. Keep the tension easy to allow for blocking, stretching, and shaping. As you work, look at your hem closely. If you are working the slip stitches too loosely, the stitches will gap and the hem will ruffle. If you are working too tightly, the bottom will draw in and the hem will not fall straight. If either of these problems is evident, rip the slip stitches back to the beginning and begin the finishing again, adjusting your tension. See illustrations at SLIP STITCHES.

Another Way to Make a Structured Hem   Cast on the number of stitches needed and work the desired hem depth. To make the turning line for the hem, knit 2 stitches together followed by a yarn-over stitch, repeating this across the row. For the next row, knit every stitch and every yarn-over stitch, for circular needles; or, for straight needles, purl every stitch and every yarn-over stitch. Continue with your garment. On straight needles, make sure you are working on the right side and that the hem will fold back to the inside. When finished, fold back on the yarn-over row and sew in place. See WEAVING for instructions on sewing a flat seam. As a final finishing, work a slip stitch in each knit stitch and chain one across each space made by the yarn-over.

A Hem Requiring No Sewing   Cast on the number of stitches needed and work the hem in the stockinette stitch for the desired depth.

ON STRAIGHT NEEDLES: With the wrong side facing you, knit 1 row. Then go back to the stitch you used for the

rest of the garment. Work even for the same number of rows as you worked on the hem. Fold the hem back, holding the bottom of the hem against the knitting on the needle. Put the right-hand needle into the first stitch on the left needle and then into the corresponding cast-on stitch at the bottom edge of the hem. Knit these 2 stitches together. Repeat this, stitch for stitch, for the entire row. Then continue with your knitting.

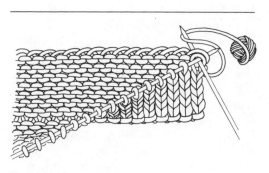

Hem requiring no sewing

ON A CIRCULAR NEEDLE: Make the hem the desired length. Then purl 1 row on the knit side. Work the same number of rows that you worked in the hem, using the stitch you will be using for the rest of the garment. Knit the hem and body together as just described.

Unstructured Hems or Borders

Hems, particularly those made of heavy yarns or those made in a stockinette stitch, roll back because they do not have a finished edge. Follow any of the procedures described here to cure this problem.

Turn the completed garment inside out and hold the wrong side facing you. Connect the yarn at the beginning of the cast-on row. Work a single crochet in every stitch, going through the entire stitch. Skip 1 stitch about every 2 inches, if necessary, to keep the edge flat. (A crochet stitch usually works out a little larger than a knit stitch. This makes it necessary to skip a stitch occasionally.) Watch to see if your hem or border is lying flat in the same way as described under Structured Hems. Turn and, with the right side facing you, work a slip stitch in every single crochet stitch.

For a deeper edge, you can continue to work in a single crochet around the bottom. You can also add a decorative border to the single crochet base row here. Finish off with the slip stitch to give the edge holding body.

Another way to finish a hem is by purling. With the right side of the completed garment facing you, connect the yarn to the beginning of the cast-on row. With a needle one size smaller than you used for the garment, pick up 1 stitch in every stitch of the cast-on row. Turn. With wrong side of the garment facing you, cast off on the purl side, using purl stitches to cast off. Always remember that casting off must be done loosely to allow the same movement to the knitted piece that it had before you added these finishing stitches.

The two following hems or borders can be worked after the garment is finished by picking up the stitches from the cast-on row and working the hem, or you can plan to make these borders or hems at the beginning of the garment when you start your knitted piece.

Garter-Stitch Border   This is one of the most popular borders. When working the garter-stitch border on circular needles, knit the first row and purl the second row; repeat these two rows until the hem or border is as deep as you like. On straight needles, knit every row to the desired depth. Use a needle one size smaller for this stitch. A garter stitch works wider than a plain stitch.

Seed-Stitch Border   In order to do this hem or border, you need an odd number of stitches on your needle if you are working on straight needles, and an even number of stitches if you are working in the round on circular needles. The instructions to follow for straight needles are: knit 1, purl 1 across the row, repeating this row for as many inches as you wish. On circular needles work:

ROW 1: Knit 1, purl 1.
ROW 2: Purl 1, knit 1.
Repeat these two rows for the hem or border.

Herringbone Pattern

Knitting in a herringbone pattern, also called *bias knitting*, produces a woven effect with a flat surface. The bottom of the knitted piece will always come out with a sawtooth or zigzag edge.

The herringbone pattern can be done on any number of stitches. The following example is based on 20 stitches.

ROW 1: Knit.

ROW 2: Purl.

ROW 3: Knit the first stitch. Pick up a stitch from the side of the stitch in the row below this stitch (an increase). Knit 7 stitches, slip 1 stitch, knit 1 stitch, pass the slip stitch over the knit stitch (a decrease), knit 2 stitches together (another decrease), knit 7 stitches, knit up to the last stitch, pick up 1 stitch from the row below the last stitch (an increase), knit the last stitch.

ROW 4: Purl, if you are using straight needles; knit, if you are working on circular needles.

Repeat these Rows 3 and 4 for pattern.

If you plan to use this pattern in a skirt or other garment that will be shaped by decreasing or increasing, plan the shaping decreases or increases to fall centered within the knit stitches of the herringbone pattern. Examining the pattern instructions for the herringbone panel, you will see that in a 20-stitch example there are two sections of 7 knit stitches each that are not affected by the increases or decreases that produce the pattern. If you are using a panel of 20 stitches, make your shaping increases or decreases in the center stitch of these 7-stitch knit sections. If the number of increases or decreases you are making in one shaping row is not enough that you increase or decrease in *every* 7-stitch part of the herringbone panel, alternate the places where you make these shaping changes so that the first time you make them in the first section of 7 stitches in the panel and the next time you make them in the second section of 7 stitches in the panel. Make sure that these decreases are made across one row, with the same number of inches between each decrease. Check on the row following the decrease row. There must be 1 stitch less (and only 1 stitch less) in that section of the panel.

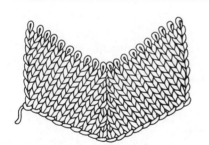

Herringbone pattern

Hoods

There are a number of ways to make hoods. Here are two.

Separate Hood

Work up a GAUGE on the yarn and needles you want to use. Multiply the number of stitches you get to the inch by 12. This will give you the number of stitches for the bottom of the hood.

Starting with needles at least 1 size smaller than those you used for the gauge, cast on the number of stitches you calculated that you need. Knit 1, purl 1 (ribbing) on the smaller needles for 1½ inches. Change to the needles you used for the gauge and work for 6½ inches. Cast off stitches equal to 3½ inches at the beginning of the next 2 rows. Work even on remaining stitches for 3½ inches. Cast off. Break the yarn.

Hood before finishing ribbing is added

FINISHING: Sew the top flat to the cast-off sides. Then, with right side of the work facing you, connect yarn at the lower right-hand edge of ribbing. With the smaller needle, pick up the number of stitches equal to 7½ inches along the side of the hood, pick up 1 stitch in each

of the cast-off stitches at the front of the hood, then pick up the same number of stitches down the other side as you did on the first side. Do a ribbing of knit 1, purl 1 for 1 inch. Cast off. Attach ties to the bottom of the hood. Make the ties out of the yarn you used to knit the hood or use ribbon or other suitable material.

Attached Hoods

If you wish to add the hood to a sweater, you can make the hood as described, but make the ribbing at the start 2 inches longer. (Instead of 1½ inches, work 3½ inches.) Pin the beginning of the ribbing to the top of the neckband of the sweater, leaving about a 6-inch opening free at the front of the neck. Weave together.

If you wish to work a hood as part of a garment rather than knitting it separately and sewing it on, when you finish the neck band of the garment cast off only the center 5 inches from the center front of the finished neck band. Then, using the remaining stitches, work the hood. Hoods of this type are usually used on cardigans, coats, or jackets and are roomier than hoods placed on sweaters. This hood will fall back and form a sort of collar effect.

Changing to a needle *at least* one size smaller than you have used for the garment, work 2 inches. Change back to the needle used for the garment. Place a marker at the center point of the stitches. If there are an even number of stitches, place the marker at the center. If there are an odd number of stitches, put a marker on the center stitch and do the shaping for the hood before and after this stitch.

To shape the hood, increase one stitch before and after the marker every inch 4 times. Work even until 6 inches from the point where you began the shaping. Then decrease one stitch each side of the marker *every row* 5 times. Cast off the remaining stitches. Fold. Sew both halves of cast-off stitches together by weaving. With right side facing, pick up stitches around the face of the hood equal to 24 inches. Cast off loosely. You can also finish off the edge around the face of the hood using crocheted SLIP STITCHES.

Increasing

Increasing is the adding of extra stitches to give shape to a knitted garment or to form a pattern. Which of the following methods should you choose for increasing? Try them all and then use the one you find most attractive to your eye or easiest to your hand.

Ways of Increasing

METHOD 1: This type of increase produces a small knot or bar on the increased stitch. It can be worked on both knit and purl stitches.

Knit the stitch on the left-hand needle from the front. Leave the stitch on the left-hand needle. Then knit the same stitch from the back. Take the stitch off the left needle. The increased stitch is the second stitch on the right-hand nee-

dle. If you are increasing a stitch on both ends of your knitting, as when you are working a sleeve, the increase at the end of the row must be done on the next-to-last stitch. To accomplish this, work to the last 2 stitches in the row. Make the

Increasing: method 1

increase in the second stitch from the end of the row in the manner described. Then knit the last stitch.

This increase does not need to be made in the first stitch at the beginning of a row. It can be made anywhere. For example, if you are increasing at both ends of a row, you can knit the first stitch and increase in the second stitch, work up to the last 3 stitches, increase in the next stitch, and knit the last 2 stitches. But always remember to make the increase one extra stitch in from the end of the row so that the little knot from the increase comes out in the same place on either side.

METHOD 2: This method gives a smoother effect. Knit the first stitch. Then, with the left-hand needle, pick up the side of the stitch on the row below the stitch you have just knitted.

Place the picked-up stitch on the left-hand needle and knit it. To increase at the end of the row, knit *up to*, but not including, the last stitch. With the right-hand needle, pick up the side of the stitch on the left-hand needle, place it on the left-hand needle, and knit it. Then knit the last stitch.

METHOD 3 (inverted increase): Knit the first stitch, pick up the yarn between the first and second stitch, and place it on the needle so the stitch faces in the same direction as the other stitches. Then knit from the back of the stitch. This twists the stitch and keeps it from making a hole.

To increase at the end of the row, raise the yarn before the last stitch and place it on the left-hand needle. Twist and knit the stitch. Then knit the last stitch.

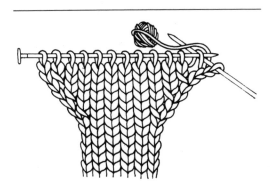

Increasing: method 3

Increasing: method 2

Increases on Circular Needles

To do increases when working on circular needles, place markers at the points where the increases go. Consider these markers equivalent to the beginning or end of a row when making the increases. Make the increase *after* a marker just as you make it at the beginning of a row, and make the increase *before* a marker just as you make it near the end of the row.

Remember that a round of knitting on circular needles is equal to a row of knitting on straight needles, and all increases to be made for that row must be made in the same round. It might seem simpler to make the first increase *before* and after the first marker in a round, but the round actually starts *at* the first marker, so make your first increase *after* it. This way, all the increasing is made in one round.

Double Increase

Here are two ways to add 2 stitches to a single stitch at one time.

METHOD 1: Knit the stitch but do not take it off the needle. Purl the same stitch, but do not take it off the needle. Knit the stitch again. Then take the stitch off the needle.

METHOD 2: Knit in the front and then in the back of two consecutive stitches.

Instructions

Determining the Correct Size

Even though you wear a size 8 in ready-to-wear clothing, you do not automatically follow the directions for the size 8

given in the instructions for the garment you are planning to knit. Sizes in knitting instructions are based on general sizing measurements, but you must take your measurements (or the measurements of the person for whom you are knitting the garment) to be sure that the size you choose to knit is the correct one.

To determine which size to knit, start by taking the bust or chest measurement (see MEASURING THE BODY). To this measurement, add 1 inch for a close-fitting garment, to allow for motion and stretch, or 2 inches for a looser fit. Check the gauge given in the instructions. Now multiply the number of stitches to the inch given in the gauge by the new chest or bust measurement that includes these new inches. Go back to the printed instructions and check which size is closest to the number of stitches you have calculated you need. If the instructions are for a garment made of pieces that will be sewn together (such as a sweater that has a front and back part), total the number of stitches given for the front and back to make this comparison.

If you are making a garment where taking the bust or chest measurement is not appropriate (for example, if you are making a skirt), take the proper measurement (the hips, in this case) and check which size is closest to the number of stitches you calculate you need at the hip.

Remember to work up a sample of knitting to make sure your GAUGE corresponds to that given in the instructions.

If you are not sure or do not feel confident about the number of stitches you are working with, the best way to feel secure is to start your garment and work up until you are 3 inches above the border. Take the stitches off the needle—don't be frightened, you can put them back on—and lay your knitting on a flat surface. Pat down. Take a tape measure and lay it across from left to right about 1 inch below the stitches you've taken off the needle.

If the piece measures a little smaller than what you had figured, but you are using wool or other natural yarn, don't worry. Natural yarns have the ability to stretch into the shape you want. It is preferable to knit garments made of natural yarn a bit narrow and a bit short. When you finish you will block your garment out to size and, if it has been knit smaller before BLOCKING, it will not stretch when you wear it.

If you are using synthetic yarns and your test piece measures smaller than you had figured, rip it out. Start again, adding the number of stitches you need, based on the gauge, to make the right size. Check the label on your yarn. It will tell you whether or not a garment will stretch when finished or if it must be knitted to size.

Having pulled the stitches off the needle, you now have to get them back on. The best way to do this is to place your right-hand needle into the stitch in the row below, pull the yarn, and then place the needle into the next stitch. Repeat until all stitches are back on the needle.

Terms

Here are six terms commonly found in knitting instructions. For explanations of the abbreviations used in instructions, see ABBREVIATIONS AND SYMBOLS.

Gauge   See discussion of this important term in the GAUGE section.

Multiple of Stitches   This term refers to the number of stitches in a pattern. When knitting directions say:

multiple of 8 stitches

it means there are 8 stitches in a pattern and that these 8 stitches will be repeated across the row. If the directions say:

multiple of 8 + 2

it means the 8 stitches are repeated across the row and you have 2 additional stitches at the end of the row to provide edges to the pattern. The multiple of stitches refers to only those stitches necessary to be repeated to make your pattern. The + stitches are the additional stitches needed to begin or end each row for your pattern to work properly as you work from one row to the next.

If you are working in a pattern and need to add or subtract stitches from those given in directions because you want to make your garment larger or smaller, you need to know what the multiple of stitches is that you are working with. If the multiple is 8 + 2, you can only add or subtract groups of 8 stitches to your work. Adding or subtracting any other number of stitches will not produce the pattern you want.

For example, after you have taken your measurements and figured out your gauge, you decide that you need 84 stitches to make your garment fit properly. Your pattern calls for a multiple of 8 + 2. Divide the 84 stitches you need by the 8 stitches of the pattern. You find you have 4 stitches over. But you need only 2 additional stitches. You can drop the 2 extra stitches from the 84 if the measurement is wide enough, working on 82 instead. If you feel that dropping these 2 stitches might make the garment too narrow, you can add 6 stitches (for a total of 90 stitches) to make the pattern work. You will then have an extra pattern and end with the 2 stitches called for in the multiple of stitches.

Pattern   A pattern is any grouping of stitches used to create a certain design. Patterns include ribs, squares, diagonal lines, herringbone, cables, textured stitches, and lacy stitches (usually called *pointelle*). A pattern can be a series of stitches that you repeat across a row, or it can be one or more rows you repeat. Or a pattern can be a group of rows repeated.

Work Even   When instructions say "work even," it means you will continue to work in whatever stitch or pattern you are using without increasing or decreasing.

Slip a Stitch   See Knit Slip Stitch under SLIP STITCHES.

Work to Correspond   This phrase is used constantly in instructions where two pieces are knitted the same but their shaping is reversed. For example, for the left front of a jacket, you work to the armhole, cast off the armhole at the beginning of a knit row, and then work to the neck. At the neck you cast off on the beginning of a purl row, shape the neck, and cast off for the shoulder at the beginning of a knit row.

Now your instructions say, "Work

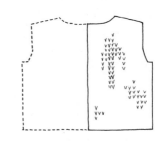

Work to correspond

right front to correspond." Here's how you do it.

Place the left front on a flat surface and try to see the corresponding front you are going to knit. If you were working the front as one piece after casting off at the beginning of a knit row for the armhole, you would finish the row, turn, and cast off at the beginning of a purl row for the other armhole. Do this for the right front, working to the underarm and casting off at the beginning of a purl row. Work to the neck; this time you cast off the stitches for the neck at the beginning of a knit row. Work to the shoulder and cast off at the beginning of a purl row.

Some knitters prefer to work corresponding pieces at the same time, using two balls of yarn. I find that the untangling of the yarn takes more time than it is worth. If is just as easy to count the number of rows on your first piece to make sure that the two pieces you knit correspond.

Adapting Patterns to Size

Let us say you find instructions for a garment with a pattern you like, but the sizes given are either too large or too small for you. What to do? Before you start to worry, take the yarn you want to use and take your required (or desired) knitting needles. First, look carefully at the instructions for the pattern (not the garment) to find out how many stitches make it up. Is the pattern made of multiples of 13 stitches or do the instructions indicate that the pattern is a multiple of 10 stitches plus 3? (The term "multiple of stitches" was explained earlier in this section.) If the instructions do not give the number of stitches in the pattern in so many words, find the part in the instructions that explains how to knit the pattern and count the number of stitches in it.

Cast on the number of stitches equal to two patterns plus, if necessary, the extra stitches needed to make the pattern work. Work up at least 4 inches and cast off. The pattern you have chosen may be stretchy, and the amount of stretch depends on the hand that knits it. Find out if the pattern as you have knitted it will stretch by dampening the swatch. Then place a wet towel over the piece and press with a steam iron. Remove the towel and pat out the steam. Let the piece dry for a few minutes and then measure how many inches you get to a pattern or how many inches you get to two patterns.

You now have to find the closest number of patterns (not stitches) that will fit the measurements you have taken. For example, you have a 13-stitch pattern and the two patterns worked up measure 5 inches (or 2½ inches to each pattern). Your back measurement is 17 inches.

Divide 17 inches by 2½ inches (the number of inches in one pattern). This gives 6.8 patterns, so you know that almost 7 patterns will make 17 inches. Since you can't knit an "almost" number of patterns, you need 7 patterns to make the back. Multiply the number of patterns (in this case, 7) by the number of stitches in a pattern (in this case, 13) and cast on (in this case, 91 stitches). If you want a loose garment, you can add an additional pattern.

Some patterns can be adapted by simply adding stitches between units. An example of such a pattern is a cable. If your measurements and your gauge indicate, for example, that you need 10 more stitches than the number of stitches given in the instructions for the largest size, divide these 10 stitches evenly between the cable patterns across the garment.

Reading Charts for Jacquard Knitting

Here is a typical chart for a pattern made up of two or more colors.

Each square represents a stitch and each mark in a square represents a color. The squares in the chart that are blank represent the main or background color of the design. If the colors that the marks on the chart correspond to are not listed below the chart, make your own list, such as:

   ✕ = red   ▲ = blue   ● = green

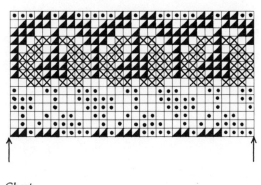

Chart

Or, if you are changing the color scheme given in the design, cross out the colors given and substitute your own choices.

On some charts you will notice arrows pointing to the outside lines of the squares. These arrows indicate the boundaries of the pattern that is to be repeated to make the design. Count the number of squares between the arrows to determine the number of stitches in the pattern. If you are altering your instructions or using the pattern to make your own design, the number of stitches you work with must be a multiple of the number of stitches in the repeat for the design to come out properly.

When you are on a knit row and are working back and forth on straight or circular needles, read the squares from right to left, starting at the bottom of the chart. Read the next row (the second row from the bottom of the chart) from left to right. When working on circular needles in the round, read all rows from right to left. To make sure that you have no holes in your work when changing colors in a jacquard design, see COLORS, CHANGING.

J

Jacquard Knitting

For advice on how to read and use the charts given for jacquard knitting, see INSTRUCTIONS. For information about working with the many colors in jacquard knitting, see under COLORS, CHANGING.

Joining or Attaching Yarn

There comes a time in all knitting when you must attach a new ball of yarn. Always add the new yarn to the side of the piece you are knitting, whether you are working in the round with circular needles or working on straight needles.

Do not join the old and new ends of the yarn by making a knot at the point where the old yarn ends if it is at all avoidable. No matter how good you think you are at hiding knots in knitting, the knot will always pop out and show.

Make sure that the end of the old yarn is at the side of a garment that is on circular needles or at the end of a row on straight needles. Rip back if necessary. Follow methods 1 or 2 to join yarn on circular needles; follow any of the methods when working on straight needles, although the last method usually works best.

METHOD 1: The yarn coming from the right-hand needle extends to the left. Take your new ball of yarn and, with its end extending toward the right, lightly twist both strands. Work 2 or 3 stitches with both ends, drop the end of the old ball of yarn, and continue working along with the new single strand.

METHOD 2: Thread the new strand of yarn into a yarn needle. Run the needle into the strand of yarn on the old ball. Pull the new yarn through. Proceed to knit.

METHOD 3: Drop the old strand of yarn. Pick up the new strand of yarn. Take the end of the new ball and tie it once around the yarn that is hanging down, making a knot. Pull the yarn up to the needle and proceed with your work. The single knot you have made can easily be worked into the seam.

Hint: How can you figure out if you have enough yarn to complete the row or enough yarn to take you to the side of the garment? I have found that it takes a length of yarn 3 times the width of the area you must cover. For example, if you have 4 more inches to knit to complete a row, you will need at least a 12-inch length of yarn. If you have worked the yarn to its very end and still have not reached the side of the knitted piece, rip back to the other side, even if the yarn you are using is expensive and you do not want to waste it.

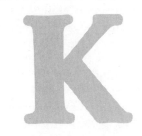

Knitting

There is more than one way to knit. No matter which way you knit, do not let anyone tell you it is the wrong way. The method you find most comfortable is the method you should use.

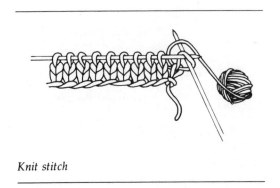

Knit stitch

The Knit Stitch

To make a knit stitch:

1. Place the right-hand needle through the front of the stitch.
2. Wrap the yarn under this needle and back over the needle, and draw this yarn through the stitch.

If your stitch falls in such a way that the needle in the front will produce a twisted stitch, place your needle into the back of the stitch, wrap the yarn over the needle in the same way, and draw the stitch through.

The Purl Stitch

The way you purl determines the way your knit stitch falls on the needle. The simplest stitch, the one easiest to increase, decrease, or work with patterns, is made by knitting from the front half of the stitch on the needle. To get a stitch to fall so you can knit it from the front, when you purl, the yarn must be in front of the knitting, positioned in front of the left-hand needle.

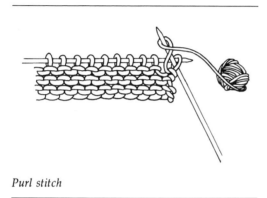

Purl stitch

Place the right-hand needle into the stitch on the left-hand needle, going from right to left. Keeping the yarn in front of both needles, place the yarn over the top of the right-hand needle. Then pull it down between the two needles and through the stitch, pulling toward the back with the right-hand needle. Drop the stitch from the left-hand needle. This method will always put the stitch on the knit side in a position to let you knit from the front.

If you put the yarn under the needle when you purl, the knit stitch will fall

in such a way that it will be hard to knit it from the front. If this is your normal way of working, knit the stitch from the back when working on the knit row. If you try to knit it from the front, it will twist and become a tight stitch in the knitted piece. Remember to check which direction your knit stitch falls on the needle when doing pattern stitches or making decreases or increases.

Uneven Knitting

If you are not getting an even, smooth surface on your knitting, it is usually because you are working one row looser than the other. The row that is looser is usually the purl row.

You can correct this problem in the following manner: For the purl row, use a needle one or two sizes smaller than the size you are using for the knit side. This will give you an even gauge. This procedure can only be followed when you are knitting on two needles. If you get an uneven stitch when working on a circular needle, try to control the yarn more evenly as you feed it into the work.

Knitting On

See CASTING ON

L

Left-handed Knitting

Knitting is done using both hands. Most right-handed knitters have to learn, at one time or another, to knit with the left hand in order to make certain patterns. It is just as simple for a left-handed knitter to work with the right hand. However, if you are left-handed and prefer not to knit as if you were right-handed, here are some hints for you.

When working on straight needles, follow the instructions for the back exactly as written. No changes are needed. Also, work a front that is made in one piece following the instructions given.

When knitting a garment that has a front opening, work in reverse—just read the instructions from right to left. For example, instructions for the right front tell you to decrease at the end of the row to shape the front. Reverse this; decrease at the beginning of the row. On the same front the instructions say to cast off 5 stitches on the purl side for the underarm. Again, reverse; cast off 5 stitches at the beginning of the knit row.

If there is to be a pocket on the left front, typical instructions read: Knit 10, cast off 12, knit 8. You will work in reverse: Knit 8, cast off 12, knit 10.

And since you are knitting from left to right, then all the patterns you have to follow will have to work in reverse.

Your main problem is to remember when and where to reverse. Some patterns do not have to be reversed. For example, cables can twist in either direction. Unless the cable is going in a certain direction for a specific reason, it really does not make any difference whether the cable goes from right to left or from left to right. However, if you want to reverse the cable, here's how.

Cable instructions that call for putting the first 3 stitches on a cable needle, holding them in front of the knitting, knitting the next 3 stitches, and knitting the 3 stitches off the cable needle can be reversed by the left-handed knitter by placing the 3 stitches in back of the work instead of the front.

To reverse other stitch patterns, follow the instructions starting from the end of the row and work backward, making sure that if the pattern is a multiple of a certain number of stitches plus additional stitches, the additional stitches are placed in their proper order at the beginning or end of the row as designated.

Some stitches, made by placing the needle in the back or in front of the stitch, are reversed by changing the place where the needle is inserted. For example, the directions to work a right twist (RT) or a right cross (RC) with the right hand would be: Knit the second stitch from the front, leave stitch on the needle, knit the first stitch, drop both from the needle. With the left hand you would: Knit the second stitch from the back, leave on needle, knit the first stitch from back of stitch, and drop both from the needle.

You must remember that patterns are sometimes made with a multiple of stitches plus what is needed at the beginning and the end of a row to make the pattern work. With some exceptions, however, most patterns can be worked from left to right as well as from right to left, *or* they can be worked by reading the instructions from the end of the row to the beginning.

Left-handed knitters need to reverse instructions for buttonholes. Where instructions call for (with the right hand) knit 2 stitches, yarn over, knit 2 stitches together, a left-handed knitter would knit 2 stitches together, yarn over, knit 2.

Lengthening

Use the same process for both lengthening and SHORTENING garments. Pull a thread from the point at which you want to lengthen the garment. Disconnect the lower portion. Pick up the stitches and knit to desired length.

Picking up stitches correctly is important if you do not want the line where you picked up the stitches to stand out. Pick up the stitches all in one direction and place them on the needle in the direction from which you will knit them. Make sure they are not twisted. See RIPPING OUT for the correct method of picking up stitches.

Lining

I do not usually recommend that a garment be lined. If it has been blocked to size it will maintain its shape. If you are lining a skirt or pants because you do not want the knitting in the back to stretch when you sit down or the knees of the pants to stretch, just remember to lift the skirt or pants slightly when you sit so that you do not pull the stitches in sitting.

To line a knit properly requires some knowledge of sewing. Cut your lining at least 1 inch wider at each seam than the knitted garment, using the knit as your pattern. Sew the parts together and then sew the lining into the garment. However, I recommend that you take your knit to a good tailor or seamstress and have it lined properly.

Loop Fringe

See under FRINGE

Looping

See Vertical Stripes under COLORS, CHANGING

Markers

See Ring Markers under EQUIPMENT

Measuring the Body

It is very important to take accurate measurements before you start a knitting project. If you are using printed instructions, check that the size you have chosen to knit is actually the correct size for your measurements. To do this, read the advice given under INSTRUCTIONS.

If you are measuring yourself, take true measurements. Don't decide the garment you plan to knit should be smaller because you are going on a diet. You might not. Or you might not lose as much as you would like to. This also applies to the measurements you take of others for whom you are knitting something. Don't let them convince you to subtract any inches from their measurements.

Following is advice and information for taking the basic body measurements needed to successfully complete most knitted garments. The letters in the Basic Body Measurement section refer to the letters in the illustration. You can find information about measuring for socks under SOCKS, for gloves under GLOVES, and for children's sweaters under BABY AND CHILDREN'S SWEATERS.

Basic Body Measurements

A. BUST OR CHEST: Remember, your bust measurement is not the same as your bra size. Take a tape measure and measure around the widest part of your bust, placing the tape a little higher when going across the back. Do not pull the tape tightly. If you prefer looser garments, add 1 to 2 inches to this measurement.

If you are full bosomed, you need more stitches at the front of the garment than at the back. You can do this in either of two ways: (1) Add the additional stitches to the front of the garment by increasing 1 stitch each side every inch, starting at the waist, until you have the number of stitches necessary. Or (2), if you want the front fuller from the waist up, increase the needed number of stitches at even intervals in the row after the ribbing or other border at the bottom. If you are making a man's sweater, add at least 1 to 2 inches to the chest measurement, since most men prefer a looser sweater, unless you know that the man who is to wear this sweater likes a tighter one.

B. SHOULDER TO SHOULDER (FRONT): This is an important measurement. It determines how deeply the underarm and armhole has to be cut so that the shoulders fit properly. You will notice that as we get older the curve at the front underarm changes. As we get older we need a deeper cutout for the front underarm.

C. SHOULDER TO SHOULDER (BACK): This measurement is taken across the back about 2 inches below the neckline.

D. SHOULDER DEPTH: Measure from the top of the shoulder to a point at right angles to a line drawn across from the underarm.

E. BACK OF NECK: Take this measurement from where the neck curves into the shoulder. This is the place where the top of a sweater or other garment will fall before a band, collar, or other finishing is added.

F. NECKLINE DEPTH MEASUREMENT: Measure this from the base of the neck to as far down as you want your neckline to be. This depth must be at least 1½ inches.

G. SHOULDER WIDTH: Measure from the base to side of the neck to the edge of the shoulder.

H. WAIST: To find the place to take this measurement, bend to the side. The place where the crease forms is the waist.

I. WAIST TO HIP: Find the widest point of your hip and then measure the depth from the waist to the hip at its widest point.

J. HIP: Measure at its widest point.

K. WAIST TO UNDERARM: Measure in a straight line from 1 inch below the armpit to the waist.

L. ARM: Measure arm from 1 inch below the armpit to the wrist. This is the sleeve length.

M. WIDEST PART OF THE ARM: Measure around the widest part at the muscle. For a comfortable fit, do not make sleeves less than 12 inches at this point, even if your measurement here is less than 12 inches.

N. WRIST SIZE: You do not measure your wrist to find out how wide the cuff of a sleeve should be; your hand must fit through the cuff before it can reach your wrist. Extend your hand in front of you. Place your thumb below your palm. Measure across your fingers and around your palm. You can make this measure a

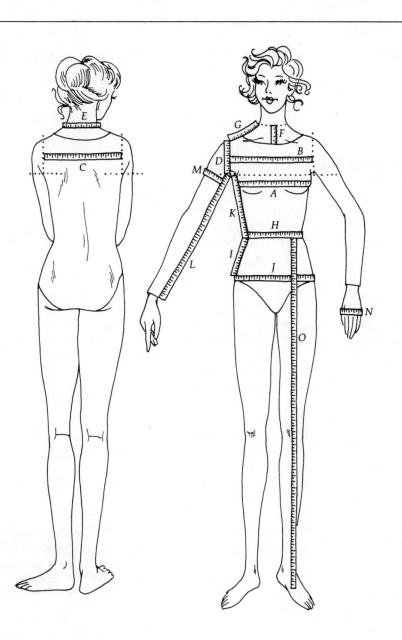

Measuring the body

little snug if you want a fitted cuff.

O. WAIST TO FLOOR: Measure in a straight line from the waist to the floor, placing the tape as close to the center front of the waist as possible.

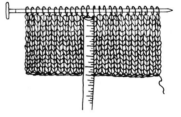

Measuring Knitting

Length   When measuring the length of your knitting when it is still on the knitting needle, place your tape measure directly under the knitting needle, not including the row on the needle, and measure down to the bottom edge. Do not skimp on this measurement. Never count the stitches on the needle as part of your work. These stitches have not been worked and are not yet part of the garment.

Always take length measurements at least 2 inches in from the edge, trying to measure down the center, if possible.

If you are knitting the back and front of a garment separately, the simplest and easiest way to make sure they are the same length is to count the nubs on the edge of the piece. Each nub corresponds to 2 rows of knitting.

When measuring the length of a sleeve, always measure from the center of the sleeve down. Measuring close to the seam edge will give you a false measurement since you will be measuring at an angle. Remember that sleeve length is measured from the underarm cast-off stitches, not from the top of the sleeve where it joins the shoulder.

Measuring length

Measuring sleeve length

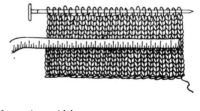

Measuring width

Width   When measuring the width of your knitting when it is still on the knitting needle, always measure at a point at least 1 inch below the needle.

When measuring for width on a garment that has ribbing on the bottom, do not measure just above the ribbing. The ribbing pulls the work in and you will not get a true measure. Work at least 3 inches above the ribbing and measure the width there.

Armhole Measurement   When measuring the depth of an armhole, measure from the shoulder to the point where you have cast off for the armhole. Place

Hip Measurements for Skirts   The best way to measure a skirt you are knitting is to try it on when you have knitted to the hip. See SKIRTS for directions on how to do this.

Stitches and Rows to the Inch   To measure the number of stitches you are knitting that make 1 inch or the number of rows that make 1 inch, see GAUGE.

Remember: Natural yarn stretches when blocked (see BLOCKING). When measuring your knitted piece, allow about 1 inch in each dimension for this stretching during blocking. Knits made with this allowance will not stretch when worn.

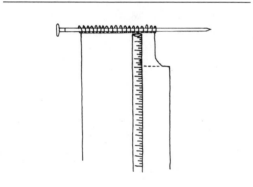

Measuring armhole depth

your tape measure under the knitting needle and measure down to the row where these cast-off stitches are. The tape measure should be at right angles to this row of stitches.

Metric Conversions

This chart shows the approximate metric equivalents for measurements useful in knitting. The metric units have been rounded to the nearest unit.

Inches	Approximate Metric Equivalent
⅛	3 millimeters
¼	6 millimeters
½	13 millimeters
¾	20 millimeters or 2 centimeters
1	25 millimeters or 2.5 centimeters
1¼	32 millimeters
1½	38 millimeters
2	51 millimeters or 5 centimeters
4	10 centimeters

Mistakes

See DROPPED STITCHES; RIPPING OUT

Mittens

Follow the same procedure as described under GLOVES, finishing the thumb and

Trying on mitten before decreasing

working the palm and the back of the glove. Do not divide stitches for the fingers but knit around until you reach the first (top) joint of the middle finger. Try the mitten on and divide the stitches by adding markers. Place one marker at each side of the hand, separating the stitches for the palm of the mitten from the stitches for the back of the mitten.

Decrease as follows: Knit up to 2 stitches before the marker. *Knit the 2 stitches before the marker together. Move the marker from the left to the right needle and slip 1 stitch, knit 1 stitch, pass the slip stitch over the knit stitch. Knit up to 2 stitches before the second marker. Repeat from * once more to finish row. Knit one row. Repeat these decreases every row around until 8 stitches remain. Finish off these 8 stitches using one of the ways described under GLOVES.

Multiple of Stitches

See under INSTRUCTIONS

Narrowing Knits

See ALTERING

Necklines

There are many kinds of necklines you can knit. The crew neck is the simplest. It falls against the base of the neck and is described under the Classic Sweater part of the SWEATER section of this book. A jewel neckline is made the same as a crew neck except that it sits about 1 inch below the base of the neck. A scoop neckline can fall anywhere from 2 to 8 inches below the base of the neck. You can find directions for these and other necklines in the following sections of this book: Scoop Neckline, Shirt-front Neckline, Square Neckline, V Neckline, Turtleneck, and Cowl Neck.

Needle Gauge

See under EQUIPMENT

Needles

Knitting needles are made of many kinds of materials: bone, steel, aluminum, plastic, wood, even bamboo. The needles described here are the ones commonly available and the ones I feel are the simplest to work with. The choice of metal or plastic lies with you. Aluminum needles make a flatter stitch than plastic needles, and plastic needles make a softer stitch than aluminum. Try both. Look at the stitch and decide which needles you like better. Some people prefer the way metal needles feel in the hand, and some prefer the softness of plastic. Use whatever you like.

Plastic needles do break, but they can be sharpened in a pencil sharpener and used for cable needles.

Needle Sizes

Knitting needles come in many sizes: from 000 to 35 in straight needles; from 00 to 13 in cable needles; from 0 to 15 in round or circular needles. The size indicates diameter of the needle, not its length (see equivalents table). The size of the needle you use depends on the yarn you plan to use and the gauge required. The smaller the needle size, the more stitches you will get to the inch. The larger the needle, the fewer stitches you will get to the inch.

Different-size needles give different effects using the same yarn. Ask yourself what effect you are looking for. If you want a tight machine-knit look, use a small needle. If you want a soft look, use a medium-size needle. If you prefer a loose, almost lacy look, use a large needle.

When working on a fine yarn, you do not necessarily use a small needle. If you have tried your yarn with a small needle but find you need fewer stitches to the inch than you are getting, move one size larger at a time until you get the number of stitches to the inch that you need.

On a medium-weight yarn, a medium-

size needle might not give you the number of stitches to the inch you need. If you want more stitches to the inch, try smaller needles. If you want fewer stitches to the inch, try ever larger needles until you get the number of stitches you want.

On a heavy-weight yarn, using a large needle, you might have the same problem. Here, too, just try a smaller needle to get more stitches to the inch or a larger needle to get fewer stitches to the inch.

Equivalents of Commonly Used Needle Sizes

American	Metric	English
—	2 mm	14
0	2¼ mm	13
1	2¾ mm	12
2	3 mm	11
3	3¼ mm	10
4	3¾ mm	9
5	4 mm	8
6	4½ mm	7
7	5 mm	6
8	5½ mm	5
9	6 mm	4
10	6½ mm	3
10½	7 mm	2
11	7½ mm	1
—	8 mm	0
13	9 mm	00
15	10 mm	000

Hint: The size needle recommended in instruction books is the needle used by the person who made the original sample garment. Each person's knitting has its own tension. Therefore, while the needles recommended are generally correct, they might not be correct for your hand. It is important that the needle you use makes the gauge called for in the instructions. If it doesn't, the garment will be either too large or too small. So feel free to experiment with needles larger or smaller, until you have your proper gauge.

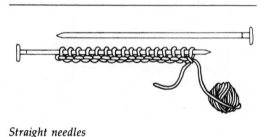

Straight needles

Straight Needles

These are needles with a point at one end. They can usually be bought 10 or 14 inches long and are made of aluminum, wood, bone, or plastic. Sizing of these needles in the U.S. ranges from 00 to 35 (from very fine to very thick). In the U.K. the needles are sized in reverse: the higher the number, the smaller the size. The 10-inch length is used for baby and children's clothes and other small items.

Short needles are also used for sleeves, mittens (when made with a seam), or hose (when made with a seam). Clothes for teenagers and adults and other larger items such as afghan strips or bedspreads made in panels are made on 14-inch needles.

Wooden needles are usually very large needles, used to knit heavy, thick yarns. With these needles you can knit a sweater in a day.

Circular Needles

Circular needles are two knitting points connected by a plastic or wire cable. In printed knitting instructions they are called circular, round, or skirt needles and are usually used to knit skirts, sweaters, coats, or any other item that can be knitted in the round without seams. Sold in 11-inch, 16-inch, 24-inch, 29-inch, or 36-inch lengths, they are made of aluminum or plastic. Although circular needles are available in an 11-inch length, I do not recommend that you use them. If you are working a number of stitches that can easily be handled by using four double-pointed needles, you'll find that it is easier to knit with the four needles than with one 11-inch needle. For average knitting, keep on hand circular needles in sizes 6 through 10½. The best length to buy is 24 inches; this length will usually work for garments most commonly knitted.

You can also use a circular needle to knit back and forth, creating an open piece rather than a tubular piece, just as you would work on two needles. For instance, you can knit a large afghan without seams. Why use a circular needle in place of two straight needles? Consider the discomfort of knitting in a chair with arms or in a narrow seat as on a plane. A circular needle instead of two long needles will solve your problem. Or, if you knit while riding in a car and don't want to keep hitting the door or the driver, again the answer is a circular needle. Another point in favor of a circular needle over straight needles is that you can't lose the other needle. And, finally, if you don't like to sew the parts of a garment together and are always looking for someone to do it for you, eliminate the seam by using a circular needle. Here's how to do it.

For a Garment That Opens down the Front   Cast on the stitches for the back and the two fronts at one time. Work back and forth just as you would on straight needles. Follow the instructions for the number of inches to the armhole. When casting off for the underarm, add the number of stitches in your instructions for casting off given for the front to the number of stitches for casting off given for the back and cast them off at one time. For example, your instructions call for 40 stitches for the back and 20 stitches for each front. Cast on 80 stitches and work up the necessary number of inches to the armhole. Your instructions now say to cast off 3 stitches on each side for underarm on the back. They also say cast off 3 stitches on the front. You would knit 17 stitches across the front, then cast off 6 stitches for the underarm (3 for the front and 3 for the back); knit 34 stitches across the back; cast off 6

stitches again for the second underarm, and knit the remaining 17 stitches for the second front. You end with the left front facing you; follow the instructions for the left front. When the left front is completed, break the yarn and follow the instructions for the right front. Then follow the instructions for the back. You have eliminated the side seams and only have to sew the shoulder and sleeve seams.

For a Pullover   Cast on the stitches for front and back at the same time, join, and work around them for the required number of inches to the armhole. Cast off the number of stitches for one side of the back underarm added to the number of stitches for one front underarm, and knit across the number of stitches required for the front of the sweater. Cast off for the other underarm similarly by adding the front and back cast-off stitches together and casting them off. Then knit across the back stitches. From this point continue working the back only, according to the instructions for the back. Begin by purling back the first row and then working back and forth as you would on straight needles. When finished with the back, break the yarn. Connect the yarn on the purl side and work the front according to instructions.

The sleeves are worked back and forth as you would on straight needles.

Hint: When working a large number of stitches on a circular needle, such as required for a skirt or dress, allow for the tendency of the knitting to be a little tighter than your gauge indicates. This happens because, when using circular needles, you do not purl back at the end of each row and you tend to pull the yarn tighter when working around and around. Therefore, when calculating the number of stitches needed, add enough stitches to equal 1 inch more than required by your gauge and size.

Remember: When joining the first row, make sure that all stitches are going in the same direction on the needle and that no stitches are twisted. After working the first round on circular needles, check again to be sure that the stitches are straight. If you don't take the time to do this, you may be unhappy later to find that your knitting is twisted. This error can only be corrected by ripping out.

When changing instructions from straight to circular needles, remember, if you are working in a stockinette stitch, to knit every row instead of knitting the first row and purling the next one. If you are working a pattern stitch and the even rows are all purl, work the even rows all knit. If the pattern calls for different stitches on every row, on the even row work the knit stitches purl and the purl stitches knit. It is best to try this out on a sample piece to see if your pattern stitch is coming out right. This table shows you the *minimum* number of stitches needed to fit around circular needles of the most common lengths. It is based on the number of stitches to the inch and the needle length. For example, if the gauge of the piece you are knitting is 7 stitches to the inch and you plan to cast on 170 stitches, select a 24-inch circular needle, since this length will

Stitches all in same direction on circular needle

accommodate over 168 stitches in this gauge. If you need fewer stitches, select a shorter needle. Too few stitches on a circular needle will make it impossible

Minimum Number of Stitches Required

Tension	Lengths of Circular Needles			
(stitches per inch)	16″	24″	29″	36″
5	80	120	150	180
5½	88	132	165	195
6	96	144	180	216
6½	104	156	195	234
7	112	168	210	252
7½	120	180	225	270
8	128	192	240	288
8½	136	204	255	306
9	144	216	270	324

for you to join the stitches and knit in the round. If you do not have enough stitches for a 16-inch needle, use a set of 4 double-pointed needles, keeping the stitches on 3 needles and knitting with the fourth.

Hint: You are making a garment that has an armhole (such as a sweater), you are using a pattern stitch, and you are working on circular needles. Where does the armhole fall in relation to the pattern? Cast off for the armhole on the *pattern row* or, if the pattern row is the first row, on any of the *odd* rows of the pattern (the third, fifth, etc.). If you don't, you'll find that your pattern will come out 1 row short or that you will be working some of the pattern stitch on the wrong rows.

When making a cable pattern, your cable twist is usually on an even row. Here, cast off on an even row for the armhole. Then, to continue working your cable on its proper row, purl back.

Double-pointed Needles

These needles have points at both ends and are usually sold in sets of 4 needles, 7 to 10 inches long. They are used to make socks, mittens, turtlenecks, and other small items knitted in the round. They can also be used to work sleeves, hats, or any other small item without seams. Circular needles cannot be used for these items because the small number of stitches they require will not stretch over the length of a circular needle. One double-pointed needle can substitute for a cable needle.

To use 4 needles, cast on the number of stitches needed on 3 needles. You can

do this by dividing the number of stitches needed by 3 and casting on each portion on a separate needle, or you can cast them all onto a single double-pointed needle and then transfer a third of them to a second needle and a third to a third needle. Join the yarn from the third needle to the first needle, using the fourth needle to work the stitches off the first needle (making sure that all your stitches are facing down). Be sure to pull the yarn when working the first two stitches of a new needle, so there is no space between the stitches.

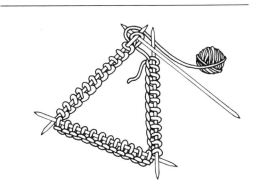

Stitches divided onto 3 double-pointed needles, with fourth needle working off first stitch

Continue knitting by taking the freed needle and knitting the stitches from the next needle. When you finish the first row, check to make sure all the stitches are going in the same direction. Check the second row also. If stitches are in the same direction after this row you will have no problem with twisted stitches later on.

P

Picking Up Stitches

Stitches are picked up along a finished edge for many purposes. You may want to make a turtleneck on a sweater; you would begin by picking up the stitches from the cast-off neckline. You are planning to add a waistband to a skirt; here you would begin by picking up the stitches from the cast-off stitches at the skirt top. You can also pick up stitches along the cardigan front to make a border.

A cast-off stitch is made of two loops, a front loop and a back loop. You usually pick up stitches from the front part of the loop. Connect the yarn at the beginning of the place where you plan to pick up the stitches, place the needle in the front loop of the cast-off stitch, and pull the yarn through. Make sure you hold the yarn firmly.

Eliminating Large Spaces   When picking up stitches for the border on the front edge of your garment or when picking up the stitches for the neck, you must make sure that you pick them up

Picking up a stitch from a loose stitch

evenly and firmly, not loosely. If you have to pick up a stitch from a loose stitch on the garment, work as follows: Pick up the yarn of the loose stitch, twist the yarn, place it on the left-hand needle, and then knit it.

(See CARDIGANS for the illustration of picking up stitches for a border, and see RIPPING OUT for picking up stitches after you have ripped out a portion of your knitting.)

Pockets

Patch Pocket

This is the simplest pocket to make. Determine how many stitches you need by counting across the stitches in the finished garment where the pocket will be placed. Cast on this number of stitches and work to the depth desired. Add either ribbing or garter-stitch border of about 1 inch. Cast off. Place on the garment and pin securely. Sew sides and bottom of pocket to the garment.

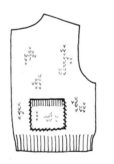

Patch pocket

Pocket Opening at the Side

For this explanation, the vertical distance from the bottom of the slit for the pocket opening to the top of the slit is called the *length* of the pocket. The *depth* of the pocket is the horizontal measurement from the pocket opening to the "bottom" or opposite end of the pocket. Also, for this example we will be making a pocket that has a slit opening that is to the left of the pocket.

1. Decide where you want the base of the slit to begin and work up to that part on the front of your garment. Work across the row up to the point where the bottom of the slit begins and place a marker here. Put the rest of the stitches on a stitch holder. Work the stitches back and forth until the slit is as long as you want it to be. This is the pocket length. Place these stitches on a second stitch holder.
2. Transfer the stitches from the first stitch holder to your needle and connect the yarn at the marker (where the slit for the pocket begins).
3. Work these stitches back and forth until the length of this section is the same as the section you have on your second stitch holder.
4. Decide how deep you want your pocket to be. Turn the garment to the wrong side. Starting at the marker at the base of the slit, count back on the same row as the marker the number of stitches equal to the depth of the pocket. Connect your yarn at this point and then pick up

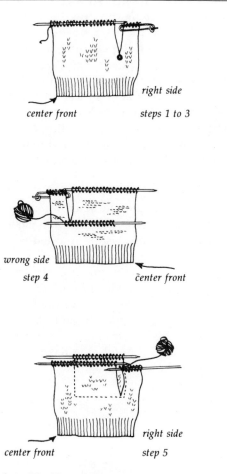

right side

center front   *steps 1 to 3*

wrong side

step 4   *cēnter front*

right side

center front   *step 5*

Pocket with side opening

are the stitches for the pocket lining. Work the pocket lining up to the same length as the length of the slit.

Now transfer the stitches still on a stitch holder to your needle and, with the right side of the garment facing you, knit the stitches until you reach the top of the slit.

5. Place the stitches from the pocket lining you have made on a double-pointed needle and hold them behind the stitches on your needle. Place your right-hand needle through the first stitch on the needle (the needle holding the stitches for the garment) and then through the first stitch on the double-pointed needle (holding the stitches for the pocket lining). Knit these two stitches together. Repeat this for the remaining pocket stitches. You have now completed the pocket. Finish your garment and sew the bottom of the pocket (the part opposite the slit) to the inside of the garment.

A pocket that opens with the slit to the right side is made the same as the one that has a slit opening to the left of the pocket, except that the stitches picked up for the lining are to the *left* of the slit on the wrong side of the garment.

Pocket with Slit Openings on Both Right and Left Sides

Decide where you want the slits for this pocket to go and work up to that part on the front of your garment. Work across the row to where the bottom of the first

the stitches across the row until you reach the slit. Then pick up one more stitch on the other side of the slit. When picking up these stitches, make sure to pick up one stitch in each stitch of the garment. These slit begins and put a marker there. Put the rest of the stitches on a stitch holder. Work back and forth until the slit is the length you want the pocket to be. Place these stitches on a second holder.

Transfer the stitches from the first stitch holder to your needle and connect the yarn at the marker. Work across the row on these center stitches to the place where the base of the second slit is to begin. Placing the last section of stitches on a stitch holder, work the center stitches until you have a piece equal in length to the first section worked. Place these stitches on a stitch holder.

Transfer the last group of stitches from the stitch holder to your needle. Connect the yarn at the base of the slit and work the last section back and forth until it is equal in length to the other two sections.

Turn your garment so that the wrong side of the work is facing you. Pick up a stitch in each stitch between the slits, including an extra stitch on either side of the slit. Work this section, which is the pocket lining, until it is the same length as the slit. Turn.

Put the stitches from the first section onto your needle and knit across them until you reach the first slit. Transfer the stitches from the middle section to another needle and put the stitches for the pocket lining on a double-pointed needle.

To connect the pocket lining to the outside of the garment, place the stitches on the double-pointed needle in back of the center stitches of the outside of the garment. Place your right-hand needle through the first stitch on the needle holding the stitches for the garment and

then through the first stitch on the double-pointed needle (holding the stitches for the pocket lining). Knit these two stitches together. Repeat for remaining pocket stitches. Transfer the stitches from the remaining last section to the needle and work across these stitches, thus finishing the row. You have now completed the pocket. Since it opens at both ends, there is no sewing down to do. Finish the rest of your garment.

Set-in Pocket

A set-in pocket should be between 4 and 6 inches deep, although you can make a deeper one if you wish. The usual width of this type of pocket is 4 inches.

Cast on the number of stitches that will produce the width of pocket you want. Work this up in a stockinette stitch or in the pattern stitch of your garment. This is the pocket lining. Knit until you reach the pocket depth you have chosen and place these stitches on a stitch holder.

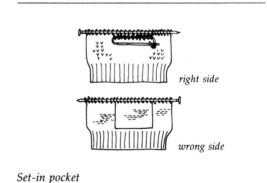

right side

wrong side

Set-in pocket

Work your garment up to the length where the top of the pocket will be. Decide where the pocket is to be placed and mark off the stitches on the garment where the pocket is to go. Place these stitches on another stitch holder. The number of stitches here must be the same as those of the pocket lining. Take the pocket lining and place it in the space where the second stitch holder is placed. Knit across the row, knitting the stitches from the pocket lining onto the needle when you come to them. Continue working on the garment.

After finishing the garment, pick up the stitches at the top of the pocket that are on the stitch holder and either work a 1-inch border in a knit 1, purl 1 ribbing or make a band in the stitch to match any borders or hem you might have. Sew the lining of the pocket in place.

Loose Pocket

A loose pocket is attached to the garment at the top only. The sides and bottom of the pocket are free.

Work the garment to the place where the top of the pocket will be. Determine how many stitches will be used for the pocket and put these stitches on a separate needle. Work on these pocket stitches for twice the depth of the pocket. Fold this flap in half and work the stitches on the pocket needle back into place with the remaining stitches on your garment.

You now have a folded flap on the inside. When you sew the sides of the flap together you will have a loose pocket. To complete, make a border at the top

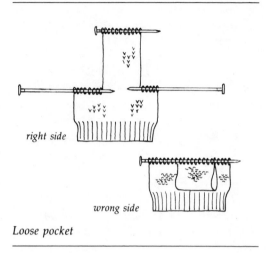

right side

wrong side

Loose pocket

of the pocket. Pick up the stitches on the outside fold of the garment (at the top of the pocket), adding 1 stitch on either side so as to avoid a hole at either end of the pocket top. Work a 1-inch border in ribbing or any other stitch you choose. Cast off and sew down the ends of the border. Sew the sides of the pocket together.

Pocket Worked as Part of Garment

Decide where you want your pocket to be placed. Work your garment up to 1 inch less than needed to reach the pocket opening. As an example, assume the gauge of your garment is 4 stitches to the inch and the pocket will be placed 2 inches in from the front edge and will be 4 inches wide. Work as follows:

Knit to the place you want your pocket to begin. In this example you knit 8 stitches (or 2 inches). Knit in a ribbing stitch for the width of the pocket. In this example, knit 1, purl 1 for 17 stitches (4 inches).

Knit the rest of the row of your garment. (If you are making pockets on each side of the garment, reverse the directions. In this example, you would knit up to the last 25 stitches of your garment, knit 1, purl 1 for 17 stitches, then knit 8.)

Work the next 3 rows, following the ribbing for the top of the pocket.

Then knit to the pocket (8 stitches) and cast off the ribbing (17 stitches), knitting over the knit stitches and purling over the purl stitches as you cast off. Work to the end of the row. (If there is a pocket at the end of the row, cast off the same way over the ribbing.) Turn.

Decide how deep you want your pocket to be. Let us say this is 5 inches. With the wrong side of the garment facing you, measure down 5 inches from the top of the pocket. Count off the same number of stitches from the edge as you worked above (8 stitches in this example). Connect the yarn on the next stitch (the ninth stitch). Then, following along on row, still on the wrong side, pick up

the same number of stitches you cast off for the pocket (17 stitches in this example). Work on these stitches for 5 inches. Then put them on the needle in place of the stitches that were cast off. Proceed with the remainder of the garment. When finished, sew the sides of the pocket to the body of the garment, making sure you do so in a straight line.

Pompoms

You can buy a pompom maker and follow the directions that come with it, or you can use one of the following two methods to make pompoms.

METHOD 1: Cut two circles of cardboard a little larger than the size you want the pompom to be at its widest part. Cut a hole in the center of each cardboard circle large enough to wrap the yarn through. A hole of 1½ inches is usually enough, but cut the hole bigger if you are making a pompom of heavy yarn.

1. Place the two pieces of cardboard one on top of the other. Wrap the yarn around them by starting at the edge, running the yarn through the center hole, wrapping it around the edge, and going through the center hole again until the cardboard is completely covered with 2 or 3 layers of yarn. Do not wrap the yarn tightly. As the hole fills up you can thread the yarn through a yarn needle to help in finishing the wrapping, but this is usually not neces-

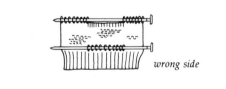

wrong side

Pocket worked as part of garment

sary if you have cut the center hole large enough. When you are finished you will have something that looks like a yarn doughnut. Break the yarn.

2. Place one point of a pair of scissors through the yarn at the edge of the cardboard and push it through so that it rests between the cardboards. Now, cut through all the yarn along the cardboard edge. Do not remove the cardboards yet.

3. Cut a piece of yarn about 6 inches long. Carefully insert it between the two cardboards. Bring it around so that it catches all the yarn going through the center of the cardboards. Tie it tightly and remove the cardboards.

4. Shake the pompom out. Using scissors, shape and trim the pompom.

METHOD 2: Decide on how wide you want your pompom and wind the yarn loosely over two, three, or four fingers, depending on the width you have selected for the pompom. Continue wrapping until the pompom is as full as you want. Do not wrap the yarn tightly.

Break the yarn. Gently remove the pompom from your fingers. Take a 6-inch length of yarn and tie the pompom securely around the center. Cut the loops on each end, shake well, and trim to shape.

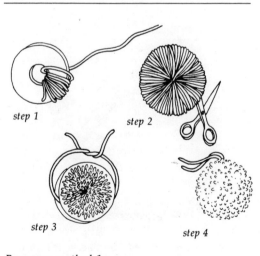

step 1

step 2

step 3

step 4

Pompoms: method 1

Ponchos

Ponchos are capes that go over the head. They can be circular or they can have four points, one centered in the front, one in the back, and one on each side over the arms. They can be made either by starting at the neck and increasing to the bottom or by starting at the bottom and decreasing to the neck.

A poncho is usually 21 inches long, 16 inches at the neck, and 120 inches at the bottom.

Circular Poncho

Here's how to make a circular poncho starting at the neck. Select yarn and needles. Start with a 16-inch circular needle at the neck and change to a 29-inch circular needle as you increase stitches. Work up a GAUGE. Check how many stitches you get to the inch and how many rows to the inch.

Let us assume that your gauge swatch shows you have 7 stitches to 2 inches (3½ stitches to the inch) and 4 rows to the inch. You need 16 inches at the neck for the poncho to go over the head. Multiply (16 by 3½) to find out the number of stitches you need to start (56).

1. Cast on the 56 stitches at a normal tension. It is very important that you not cast on too tightly. The neckline needs to have normal tension so that it will expand and go easily over the head. Knit the first row around, thereby connecting the first and last stitches to make a circle.
2. Next, to figure how many stitches you need at the bottom to make 120 inches, multiply your gauge of 3½ stitches to the inch by 120 inches. This tells you that you need 420 stitches at the bottom.
3. Now figure out how many rows you have in which to increase from 56 stitches to 420 stitches; that is, to add 364 stitches. Allowing 1 inch for stretching in blocking, multiply the length (20 inches) by 4 rows to the inch. This tells you that you have 80 rows in which to do your increasing.

You do not want to add stitches every row; this would make the poncho ruffle. But you can add stitches every other row if you do not add too many at one time, which gives you 40 rows (every other row) in which to add 364 stitches. If you

divide 364 stitches by 40 rows, you get 9 and a couple of extra stitches. This means you can increase 9 stitches every other row for 40 rows. Make these increases as evenly spaced as possible. Then work even until the poncho is long enough. Cast off very loosely.

You can finish off the edges with FRINGE or add a crocheted or knitted edge (see HEMS). The neck can be left as is, or you can loosely crochet a row of slip stitch or single crochet around to finish it (see Edges under FINISHING). You can also pick up the stitches and knit a collar or a turtleneck.

Poncho with Four Points

For a poncho made with 4 points, let's use the same gauge and dimensions as the circular poncho for our example. Cast on 56 stitches. Place a marker after each 14 stitches. You will have 4 markers,

Markers on circular needle for poncho with four points

which are your 4 increase points. Increase 1 stitch before and 1 stitch after each marker, *every other* row, 45 times, until you have 416 stitches. Work even until the desired length. Cast off loosely. Finish with fringe, if desired, or add a crocheted or knitted border. Finish the neckline as described for the circular poncho.

Pulls or Snags

Your knit catches on something and you have a pulled loop a few inches long. You think it is ruined. Not so. As soon as you can, remove the garment and look at it (calmly, if possible) to see what has happened.

The yarn will have pulled, either from one side only or from both sides. A small crochet hook or the point of a yarn needle can be used to repair this. One side of the pull might be longer than the other. Count the number of stitches pulled on either side. Look at the length of the loop. Pick up the yarn needle and trace the stitches to see which way you have to move the yarn in the loop to put it back into place. With the needle, pick up the yarn of the first stitch pulled near the loop. Gently ease the loop yarn back

into the stitch up to the point you think is necessary to fix that side. Follow the stitch and ease the yarn back into the other half of the stitch. Continue this way until you have loosened up all the stitches that were pulled on one side. Then do the same thing for the other side.

If the yarn broke when snagged, find a piece of yarn to match and tie it to both ends of the broken yarn. Then loosen the pulled stitches as described. Pull the ends of the yarn to the wrong side and tie two knots, as small and soft as possible. The new yarn serves to connect the ends of the broken yarn and usually will appear only on the wrong side. Work in the ends of the yarn, and your garment is whole again.

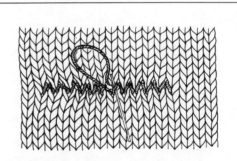

Pulling snagged yarn back in place with yarn needle

Raglan Sleeves

Raglan sleeves extend from the bottom of the sleeve to the neckline of a sweater, dress, or coat, with the sides of the sleeve slanting from the underarm to the neckline. A raglan sleeve, by its shape, requires a deeper armhole for it to fit properly, and both the body of the garment and the raglan sleeves themselves are made fuller to allow for the raglan shape. Raglan sleeves can be knitted separately and woven into the garment. Or the sleeve seams can be eliminated entirely by knitting the sleeves and the body of the garment all in one piece, using circular needles. There are two methods for making raglan sleeves without seams on the yoke of the garment. You can work the garment from the neck down, making increases for the raglan at the sleeve seam line, or you can work the back, front, and sleeves of the garment separately up to the armhole, joining them on a circular needle and making the decreases at the sleeve seams to the neckline.

The most important thing to remember when making a raglan sleeve that is to be sewn into the body of the sweater is

Sweater with raglan sleeve

that you *must* have the same number of rows from the armhole to the neck on the back, front, and sleeves for the sleeve to fit properly. This does not mean that you will have the same number of decreases on each section all the time. Some designs require a fuller body or a slimmer body, and some designs require tighter sleeves.

In the following explanation, we will work with a sleeve that is knitted separately from the cuff up to the neckline, and where the slant on the sleeve will be made by decreasing. Be sure to distribute these decreases properly to make all sections come out even. Here's how.

As an example, assume that the instructions for your sweater indicate that on your last row before casting off there must be 10 stitches for the back, 5 stitches for each shoulder, and 12 stitches for the front (ignoring any shaping for the neckline here). Before the first raglan decrease, you have on your needles 42 stitches for the back, 31 stitches for each sleeve, 48 stitches for the front.

To figure out how to make the decreases for the raglan, you first determine how many rows you have in which to make them—how many rows between the armhole and the neckline. The average depth for the armhole in a woman's raglan sleeve is 9½ inches, and we will use this 9½-inch figure in the calculations. But remember to take your own measurements by measuring from the top of the neck down to the armhole, measuring at right angles to the armhole (see MEASURING THE BODY), adding an extra inch for the fullness required in the raglan.

Your gauge shows that you get 4 rows to the inch. That means you need 38 rows (9½ times 4) for your armhole and you have to end up with 10 stitches for the back, 5 stitches for each shoulder, and 12 stitches for the front. Each time you decrease you are decreasing one stitch on each side of each piece—the back, the front, and each sleeve—a total of 2 stitches per decrease row per piece, or 8 stitches in every decrease row. Make a table showing the number of stitches you have left after each decrease row, like this:

Back	Front	Sleeves
42	48	31
40	46	29
38	44	27
36	42	25
34	40	23
32	38	21
30	36	19
28	34	17
26	32	15
24	30	13
22	28	11
20	26	9
18	24	7
16	22	5
14	20	
12	18	
10	16	
	14	
	12	

Count the number of decrease rows in the table. There are 16 knit rows for the back, 18 knit rows for the front, and 13 knit rows for the sleeves. (You need 2 rows for each decrease: The first row is the knit row, the row you decrease on; the second row is the purl-back row.)

Remember we figured we needed 38 rows or 19 knit rows for the 9½-inch armhole. You see from the table that you can accomplish all the decreases for the back in 16 knit rows, but you need a total of 19 knit rows to make the sleeves fit properly. You do this by first decreasing on every *second* knit row 3 times for the back to spread the decreases over 19 rows instead of 16. Decrease on the second knit row just 1 time for the front in order to extend the 18 rows to the required 19 rows. Decrease on every second knit row 6 times for the sleeves to extend 13 rows to 19 rows.

Now you know that you knit the back by decreasing 1 stitch each side every second knit row 3 times and then every knit row until 10 stitches remain. For the front, decrease 1 stitch each side on the second knit row once, then decrease on every knit row until 12 stitches remain. For each sleeve decrease 1 stitch each side every second knit row 6 times, then decrease every knit row until 5 stitches remain. This gives you the correct number of decreases on the necessary number of rows.

Working Raglan Sleeves as One Piece with Garment

Knitting from the Armhole up to the Neckline Work the front and back of the garment up to the armhole and work the raglan sleeves up to the armhole, following your instructions. Cast off the required number of stitches for each piece for the underarm shaping. Now you are going to put all these pieces on a circular needle. Where to start?

First, make sure that you have ended each piece by purling back the last row so each piece is ready to be worked starting on the knit or right side. This will enable you to start all pieces by knitting the first row. If you are knitting a cardigan, place your knitting on the circular needle as follows: right front, sleeve, back, sleeve, left front. For a pullover, place the pieces on the needle in the following way: back, one sleeve, front, second sleeve. Place a marker between each section. For the pullover, place a different color marker between the second sleeve and the back. This will mark the beginning and end of a row on the pullover, the back being the beginning of the row and the second sleeve being the end of the row.

It is best to get all your stitches on the needle before starting to knit so that you can more easily follow any instructions you may have. Some patterns call for specific things to be done on the first row. Therefore, if you put all your stitches on the needle, you can proceed with the instructions as given or you can follow the method just explained for planning your raglan sleeve.

TO MAKE THE DECREASE FOR THE RAGLAN: Always work the stitches *after* the marker, as follows: Slip the first stitch as if you are going to knit it, knit 1, pass the slip stitch over the knit stitch. Work up to the last 2 stitches *before* each marker and then knit these 2 stitches together. Making the decreases in this way will produce decrease stitches that slant toward each other, rather than both slanting in the same direction (see discussion at DECREASING).

TO EMPHASIZE THE RAGLAN: After the marker, knit 1, slip 1, knit 1, pass slip stitch over knit stitch; work to last 3 stitches; knit 2 together, knit 1 before marker.

TO EMPHASIZE THE RAGLAN EVEN MORE: Knit 2, slip 1, knit 1, pass slip stitch over knit stitch after marker; work to last 4 stitches; knit 2 together, knit 2.

Note: You can change the number of stitches before and after the marker for your raglan only if you are doing a stockinette stitch with no pattern. Patterns have to be followed, and changing the number of stitches used for your raglan might not work for a knitted piece that has a pattern stitch.

Knitting from the Neckline down to the Armhole   In garments where the knitting begins at the neck instead of the bottom, the sleeves are usually knitted together with the body of the garment. The increases are worked in the places where the sleeve would have been sewn in if it had been knitted separately. Any of the methods described for INCREASING can be used to work these increases.

As an example, let us say you need 36 stitches at the neck divided as follows: 12 stitches for the back, 16 stitches for the front, and 4 stitches for each sleeve. Cast on and knit one row. Place markers between each section; the row begins at the back with the 12 knit stitches. Using

the method of increasing by knitting the stitch from front and back, work as follows:

ROW 1: Increase in the first stitch and knit to within 2 stitches of the next marker; increase, knit 1 stitch, slip marker; increase stitch after the marker; knit to last 2 stitches before next marker; increase, knit 1 stitch, slip marker; increase, knit up to last 2 stitches before next marker; increase, knit 1 stitch, slip marker; increase, knit to last 2 stitches before next marker; increase, knit 1.

ROW 2: Knit all stitches.

This gives you 8 added stitches in one row. It adds one stitch on either side of the front, one stitch on either side of each sleeve, and one stitch on either side of the back. Repeat these two rows, increasing 8 stitches in one row and knitting straight on the second row, until the raglan reaches the desired length to underarm.

Hint: A raglan sleeve for a man's sweater should be at least 11½ to 14 inches measured along the slant at the outer edge of the raglan. (This is the measurement from the underarm seam to the shoulder.) Or the raglan should be at least 11 inches measured straight from the underarm to the shoulder. (This measurement is at right angles to the stitches cast off at the underarm.) The dimension for a woman's raglan sleeve, as described in the preceding discussion, is 9½ inches.

Repairs

See GRAFTING; PULLS OR SNAGS

Ribbon

Knitting with ribbon requires a different technique from knitting with yarn. When making a knit stitch in ribbon, insert the needle through the back of the loop and wrap the ribbon forward over the needle. This is the reverse of what you usually do. Make the purl stitch in the usual way. Try to keep the ribbon flat on the needle when working. A tug on the ribbon will usually make it straighten out.

To keep the ribbon from twisting as you pull it from the spool, poke holes on opposite sides of a box big enough to hold the ribbon spool, such as a shoe box or an old gift box. Insert a knitting needle, pencil, or anything long and smooth into the hole on one side. Put the spool of ribbon on the needle (or whatever you are using) inside the box. Then put the needle through the other side of the box. The spool will turn on the needle. This helps to eliminate most of the twisting, but not all. When it is necessary to untwist the ribbon, remove it from the box, pin the ribbon to the spool so that it will not unwind, and allow the spool to hang down until the ribbon is untwisted. Place it back in the box and continue.

Work very loosely. Unravel a long length so that there is no tension on the ribbon.

If you have to rip, make sure you press the ribbon before using it again.

To block, push the fabric together slightly so that it will give more of an interwoven effect. Cover with a damp cloth and steam thoroughly. Test a piece of ribbon beforehand to make sure the temperature is not too hot for the ribbon.

Be sure to make a gauge swatch with your ribbon and block the gauge swatch. After blocking you will find you have fewer stitches and rows to the inch than you had in the unblocked piece. The quality of the ribbon influences how much shrinkage there is. Make sure to allow for this shrinkage when figuring out the number of stitches you need and the length to knit.

Ring Markers

See under EQUIPMENT

Ripping Out

Unfortunately, you will find occasions when you need to rip out your knitting—you've made an error, changed your mind about the pattern you want to use, decided to change the style of the neckline, or any of a number of other reasons.

You should also consider ripping out a portion of your knitting when you have let it sit for a week or two. If you continue to knit on something that has been put aside, you will find that the first row you knit off the needle will look different from your regular knitting. This happens because the yarn has taken on the shape of the needle while waiting to be knit. This creates a ripple in the knitting, a ripple that should be removed. To remove the ripple, leave the stitches on the needle and put the point of the needle going from the back of your knitting toward the front (toward yourself) into the first stitch in the row below. Gently pull the yarn out of that stitch, dropping the stitch from the needle in your left hand. Follow this procedure with your right-hand needle and rip out at least 1 row. In some cases (you can tell by how much of a ripple there is in the yarn) it is best to go back 2 rows. Break off the rippled piece of yarn and join a new piece.

Picking Up Ripped-out Stitches

This procedure can be used anywhere you have ripped-out stitches. Take the knitting off the needle and rip down to where you want to begin again. If you are correcting an error, rip down to the row that contains the error. Take your knitted piece in your left hand and your needle in your right hand. Put the point of the needle going from the back of your knitting toward the front (toward yourself) into the first stitch in the row below. Gently pull the yarn out of that stitch. Now, the same way, place your

needle into the next stitch in the row below and gently pull the yarn. Continue this until all the stitches are on the right-hand needle. By placing the needle into the stitch before ripping the final row, you keep the stitch from dropping.

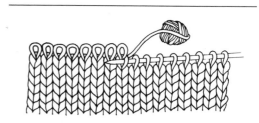

Picking up ripped-out stitches

Hint: In a pattern stitch there frequently is an all-knit or all-purl row. When ripping a pattern, make sure the last row you rip is the row above the all-knit or all-purl row. Then, with the wrong side of garment facing you, pick up the stitches in the manner just described.

Row Counters

See under EQUIPMENT

Ruler

See under EQUIPMENT

S

Scarves

Scarves can be lovely, unusual and colorful but, for a new knitter, very boring. Fashion has made scarves from 4 to 12 inches wide and from 30 to 80 inches long. The average scarf for under a coat is 6 to 8 inches wide.

Scarves can be made of any type of yarn. You can use a fine, medium, or heavy yarn or a combination. Mixing yarns can create interesting effects. When choosing a stitch for your scarf, remember that you see both sides of a scarf when it is worn, so choose a stitch that looks good on both sides. Or you can use a circular needle to make a tubular scarf of a fine yarn where you need not be concerned about the right and wrong sides of the stitch.

Recommended: Although scarves are simple to knit, if you are a beginner, don't make a scarf your first project. A scarf takes a long time to finish and doesn't teach you much except how to work the stitch you've chosen. But make a scarf when you want one for yourself or someone dear to you, knowing that the steadier you work on it the faster you will get through.

Scoop Neckline

A scoop neck curves deeply into the front of the garment. The bottom curve of a scoop neck can be anywhere from 2 inches from the base of the neck to armhole level, or about 8 inches from the base of the neck. The shape of the scoop can also vary, since the base of the curve can be made from 2 to 6 inches across.

Sweater with scoop neckline

The shoulder seam of a sweater or other garment made with a neckline where the base of the neckline rests at the base of the neck (as for a crew neck) is usually 4 inches. Shoulder seams on tops with a scoop neck are shorter, usually 2½ inches, since the top of the scoop does not rest at the base of the neck. So, when making a scoop neckline, make sure that you work the stitches at the back of the garment so that the number of stitches left for the shoulder equals 2½ inches. As an example, if you are working with a gauge of 4 stitches to the inch, leave 10 stitches at each shoulder.

For this example we will also assume that the measurement from shoulder to shoulder is 12 inches (see MEASURING THE BODY). This means that there would be 48 stitches on your needle after you have cast off stitches for and shaped the armhole (12 inches times 4 stitches to the inch). You need 2½ inches—10 stitches—at each shoulder, or a total of 20 stitches. Subtracting the number of stitches needed at the shoulders (20) from the number of stitches you have from shoulder to shoulder (48) leaves 28 stitches—the number of stitches you can work for the scoop neckline.

Let us make the scoop neckline 4½ inches across at the base. Work across the row where the base of the neckline is to fall and cast off the center 18 stitches (4½ times 4 stitches to the inch). Then, working one side of the neck at a time, decrease 1 stitch at the neck every other row 5 times. This means that you knit 2 stitches together at the neck edge at the beginning of a knit row when working on the left side of the front and that you purl 2 stitches together at the end of the purl row when working on the right side. Work each side even until the front is the same length as the back up to the shoulder. Cast off.

To finish the neckline, use a circular needle one size smaller than the needle size used to knit the garment. With the right side of the work facing you, connect the yarn at the right side of the back of the neck. Pick up the stitches across the back, skipping every fifth stitch (to draw in the back of the neck). Then pick up the stitches along the side of the left shoulder. Pick up a stitch in each of the 5 decreased stitches. Pick up the stitches across the front cast-off stitches, skipping at least 2 stitches to draw in the neckline so it lies flat. Then pick up the same number of stitches along the right side of the neck as you picked up on the left side of the neck. **Simple Edge**   Knit 1 row around. Cast off up to the last stitch. Do not break the yarn but proceed to pick up 1 stitch in the front of every cast-off stitch all around. Turn. With the inside of the neckline facing you, cast off all stitches from the purl side, purling each stitch as you cast off.

Picot Edge Knit 1 row around. For the second row, *yarn over, knit 1*; repeat around row. Knit 1 more row and cast off.

Ribbed Edge Knit 1, purl 1 for 1 inch. Cast off.

Collar With the wrong side of the garment facing you, connect the yarn at the right corner of the back of the neck. Pick up following the method just described under how to finish the neckline. Using a needle a size smaller than you used for the garment, begin the collar as follows:

Knit 1, purl 1, increase next stitch; repeat between asterisks for one row. Follow the ribbing of this row, knitting over the knit stitches and purling over the purl stitches, for three rows. Then change to a needle of the size used for the body of the garment and continue ribbing for at least 4 inches. Cast off loosely.

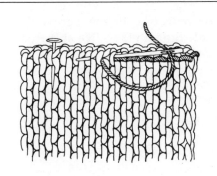

Back-stitch seam

Seams

For those who do not like to weave seams, the following seams are suggested.

Back-stitch Seam

Place the two pieces to be joined with their right sides together, facing each other, and their wrong sides out. Use large pins, such as bank pins, perpen-dicular to the seam line to hold the pieces in place. Thread a yarn needle and, starting at the lower right-hand corner, connect the yarn at the edge by pulling the yarn through the nub at the end of the knitted row. Make a stitch through both pieces ⅛ inch in from the edge. With the needle at the back of the work, bring it up through the front and go to the right for the length of 1 stitch. Put the needle through to the back and, going to the left, make 1 more stitch, approximately the same length as the first stitch made. End the stitch with the needle in the front. With the needle in the front, go back 1 stitch to the right, down to the back of the work, up at the end of the last stitch, and repeat to end of seam. Work in the loose end as described under FINISHING.

Overcast or Flat Seam

Place the two pieces to be joined next to each other with their right sides facing.

Thread a yarn needle and connect the yarn to the edge of one piece. Put the needle through the stitch at the edge of this piece and then through the corresponding stitch on the edge of the other piece. Keep the needle in a direction so that it is going toward you (from underside of work to front) as you sew this

Overcast or flat seam

stitch. Go through the next stitch on the first piece and then into the corresponding stitch on the second piece with the needle pointing away from you (from topside of work to back). Continue in this way until the seam is completed.

For information about yarn for sewing seams, see under WEAVING.

Selvedge Stitches

Selvedge stitches are extra stitches worked at the beginning or end of a row to make an edge that may be joined with another later or left open in the finished garment. Although edges with selvedge stitches are difficult to weave together, some knitters prefer the way a seam or edge with selvedge stitches looks. So, for those knitters, here are half a dozen selvedge edges.

SELVEDGE 1: This is a simple selvedge. All you need to do is always knit the first stitch of every row.

SELVEDGE 2: This selvedge is usually used when working the garter stitch. Holding the yarn in front of the garment, slip the first stitch as if you are going to purl. Then knit the rest of the row. Repeat at the beginning of every row.

SELVEDGE 3: This selvedge is used when working the stockinette stitch. On the first row, slip the first stitch as if to knit. Knit the rest of the row and turn. On the second row, slip the first stitch as if to purl. Purl the rest of the row. Repeat these rows.

SELVEDGE 4: This selvedge is also used with the stockinette stitch. On the first row, slip the first stitch. Knit the row up to the last stitch and slip this last stitch, leaving the yarn in front of the work when you turn. Purl across the next row, purling the first and last stitch you slipped in the row before. Repeat these rows for the selvedge.

SELVEDGE 5: This is a more complicated selvedge edge. On the first row (knit side), slip the first stitch as if to knit. Purl the second stitch. Knit up to the last 2 stitches. Purl the next stitch and slip the last stitch as if to knit. Turn and purl back the entire row. Repeat these rows for the selvedge.

SELVEDGE 6: Knit across the first row up to the last stitch. Slip the last stitch and turn. Purl back the next row up to the last stitch. Slip the last stitch. Repeat these rows for the selvedge.

Sequins

Threading the Sequins   Using a regular sewing needle, take a piece of sewing thread about 10 to 12 inches long. Fold it in half and thread the two loose ends through the eye of the needle. Take the end from the ball of yarn you are using and pull it through the loop at the end of the sewing thread, letting about 6 to 8 inches of yarn hang loose. Thread the sequins onto your knitting yarn by slipping the sequins onto the needle, onto the sewing thread, and, finally, onto the yarn. Pull the sequins down as far as necessary into the ball of yarn to accommodate all the sequins you think you will use in knitting your garment.

Knitting the Sequins   Whenever you are going to add a sequin to the garment, slip the sequin close to the work. Knit the stitch where the sequin is to go from the back of the loop, pushing the sequin through the stitch to the front of the work.

Shawls

You can make a simple rectangular shawl just like a scarf, only wider. Shawls are intended to cover the shoulders and the upper arms; make them at least 15 inches wide and at least 55 inches long—longer if you prefer.

The selection of yarn for a shawl is purely personal. For a dressy shawl you might choose a lightweight yarn. For cool evenings, choose something a little heavier. You can use almost any stitch for a shawl.

V-shaped Shawl

Select your yarn and needles, choose the stitch you want to use, and make a sample GAUGE. Decide how long you want your shawl to be. Multiply this length by the number of stitches to the inch in your gauge and cast on an even number of stitches. Divide the number of stitches in half. Place a marker on the needle at the center.

ROW 1: Work even (no increases).
ROW 2: Increase the first stitch. Work up to 2 stitches before the marker. Slip 1 stitch, knit the next stitch. Then pass the slip stitch over the knit stitch and drop from the needle. Move the marker from the left-hand needle to the right-hand needle, knit 2 together, work up to the last stitch, increase this stitch.

Repeat these two rows until the shawl is the desired width.

Shirt-front Neckline

A neckline that looks like a shirt opening can be started as low as the row on which you do your casting off for the armhole. If you prefer an opening that is not so deep, work for up to 3 inches from the armhole before starting this neckline. For this example, let us assume there are 56 stitches for the front on the needle at the point where you want the shirt neckline to begin (28 stitches for each half) and also let us assume that the gauge is 4 stitches to the inch.

Sweater with shirt neckline

RIGHT FRONT: Work the right front first. To do this, purl across 26 stitches (on the wrong side) and then work 4 more stitches. These 4 centered stitches are used for the band. Keeping these 4 stitches in the border stitch you select for this garment, work up the 30-stitch right front until it is 1½ inches less than the back.

Here, as in the classic sweater (under SWEATERS), we are assuming you need 16 stitches (4 inches) for the shoulder. In order to give the front neckline the proper curve to round the neck, you need 3 additional stitches for the shaping. Subtracting these 19 stitches for the shoulder and neckline from the 30 stitches on the needle leaves 11 stitches. Cast them off at the neck edge and finish the row. Then decrease one stitch at the neck edge every row 3 times. This shapes the neck into a soft curve. Now measure the front against the back. If the front of your sweater is not as long as the back to the shoulder, knit until it is as long. Cast off 8 shoulder stitches from the armhole side, going toward the neck, every other row 2 times.

LEFT FRONT: To work the left front, connect the yarn on the purl side inside the 4 stitches of the border. Pick up 1 stitch in each of these 4 stitches and continue purling across the row. Work to match the right front, shaping the neck in the same way. Cast off for the shoulders.

Neckline Finishes

To finish off the shirt-front neckline you can add a band of ribbing, finish with a stockinette hem, or make a small collar.

Ribbed Band   Hold the garment with the right side facing you. Connect the yarn to the right corner of the neck edge and pick up enough stitches to equal 15 inches around the neckline. (Using the example gauge of 4 stitches to the inch, you would pick up 60 stitches evenly around the neckline.) Make a ¾- or 1-inch band of ribbing using a knit 1, purl

1 rib pattern. Cast off, remembering to cast off the knit stitches by knitting and the purl stitches by purling.

Stockinette Hem   Pick up stitches as described in the preceding paragraph, but a number only equal to 14 inches. You pick up fewer stitches here because a flat hem made in a stockinette stitch tends to work out a little wider than a rib stitch.

Work in a stockinette stitch to whatever depth you prefer; I usually work a ¾-inch band. Purl 1 row on the knit side of the band. Go back to the stockinette stitch and work 1 row less than you worked on the first part before the purl row. Cast off loosely. Turn the edge back on the purl row and weave into place.

Collar   Hold the garment with the wrong side of the left front facing you. Pick up a number of stitches equal to 15 inches. Purl back the row.

The simplest way to make a collar is to increase 1 stitch in every third stitch across the next row. Make this row of increases and then decide if you want the ends of the collar to be pointed or rounded. For pointed ends such as you'd see on a shirt, work the collar 3 to 4 inches or the depth you desire, increasing 1 stitch at each end of every other row. Cast off loosely.

If you prefer a rounded collar, work even for 2 inches. Then decrease 1 stitch at the beginning and end of each knit row 2 times and then at the beginning and end of every row (both knit and purl rows) 5 times. Cast off loosely.

If you want a blunt-edge collar, as shown in the drawing, work the same way you would for the pointed collar but

do not increase at the ends of the row. Work 3½ to 4 inches. Cast off loosely.

Shortening

Something you made last year is too long, or you lost weight and your skirt has dropped to a longer length. With a pin or a piece of contrasting yarn, mark the new length you have chosen on your garment. Using a large pin or needle, pick up a stitch on a row that is 2 rows below the row you have marked. Lift the stitch and pull it out. (You've seen a stitch pulled like this when you snagged a sweater on a nail, but now you are deliberately pulling the yarn.) Pull the yarn as far as it will go. It will get tight and the stitches will bunch together. Break the yarn and smooth out the gathers. The pieces will separate. Find the end of the broken yarn and pull again. Repeat until the two pieces are complete-

Pulling yarn to separate pieces for shortening

ly separated, but do not break the yarn the last time.

Using a knitting needle the same size as the one used for the garment or a size smaller, and holding the right side of the garment facing you, place the needle in the stitch in the row below the ripped row. With your other hand pull the yarn. In this way you are picking up stitches while pulling out a row. Repeat until you have picked up all the stitches. Go back to the needle used to knit the garment. You can now finish the edge so it is the same as it was before, or make a new edge. For some suggestions see HEMS.

The same method can be used to shorten a sweater with ribbing. Here you add the depth of the ribbing to the amount you want to shorten the sweater. If your ribbing is 3 inches and you want to shorten your sweater 2 inches, mark your edge 5 inches from the bottom. Pull out the thread as just described and pick up the stitches. Knit back the 3 inches of ribbing (see Reusing Yarn under YARN).

Side-to-Side Knitting

You can create many interesting versions of a simple garment merely by changing the direction in which it is knitted. Usually, a knitted garment is worked from the bottom up. Side-to-side, or vertical, knitting is accomplished by knitting from one side of the garment to the other. The rows of knitting are vertical rather than horizontal, and interesting

striped effects are created. Side-to-side knitting is especially effective when done in the garter stitch, but the stockinette or any other stitch can be used. Sweaters, skirts, coats, and scarves are a few of the items that can be knitted this way. See SKIRTS for directions for side-to-side knit skirt; see SWEATERS for a sweater knitted from sleeve to sleeve.

Skirts

There are two basic styles for skirts that withstand style changes: straight and A-line. These also are styles that can easily be lengthened or shortened to fit the vogue of the year. When buying yarn for a skirt, buy some extra yarn to allow you to make alterations.

First, take your measurements (see MEASURING THE BODY). These must be accurate. Measure your waist and hips at their widest point and determine the skirt length you would like. To do this, take a skirt of the right length and measure it from the top of the waistband to the hem, along the center back. Subtract 1 inch to allow for stretch in blocking.

Measure the waist loosely. Getting the waist too small will make it difficult to put the skirt on.

Measure the hips at their widest point. This hip measurement (for shaping the skirt) is usually 9 to 10 inches down from the waist. Do not figure that you will be smaller when the skirt is finished. Take your true measurements. For the proper width at the bottom of the skirt, add 10 to 14 inches to the hip measurement.

Skirts are usually knitted from the bottom up on circular needles. The idea that a professional-looking skirt must have seams is just not so. If you like a skirt with seams, fine, but seams are not necessary. If your yarn is going to give in either the length or the width, the seams contain and restrict the natural elasticity of the yarn and you will have a skirt that sags, especially in the back. If you prefer seams in a skirt, join the sections by WEAVING. That will help avoid sagging.

Hint: The best way to measure a skirt as you are knitting it is not to measure it on a flat surface but to try it on. Work the skirt to the hip. Take the needle out of the skirt. (Don't panic: You will only lose one row when you pick the stitches up again.) Slip the skirt on. Let the top reach the hip. The skirt should not be too tight or too loose. Put the stitches back on the needle (see Picking Up Stitches under RIPPING OUT). If the skirt fits comfortably, continue decreasing as planned. If the skirt feels a little large, you will have to decrease more stitches between the hips and the waist. Plan to add 2 more decrease rows than you had originally planned for the area between the hips and the waist. This means you will decrease more often and the decrease rows will be closer than you had originally planned for this part of the skirt. If the skirt feels a little snug, do not make as many decreases from the

hips to the waist as you had planned, remembering to space the decrease rows evenly.

Straight Skirt

This skirt is a simple one, but, despite its name, it is not made with the same number of stitches from the bottom up. A straight skirt needs at least 10 inches more width at the hem than at the hip.

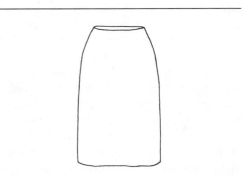

Straight skirt

With the yarn you intend to use, cast on 20 stitches and work them up into a square, using the stitch you have chosen for the skirt. This is your GAUGE sample.

To start, take your hip measurement (for this example, 38 inches) and add 10 inches for walking room (the measurement of the width at the bottom, or hem). Multiply the number of inches in the hem (48 inches) times the number of stitches your gauge shows you have in an inch (for this example, 4 stitches):

here, 192 stitches. Then add at least the number of stitches equal to 2 inches to the total to allow for the slight pulling in that takes place when knitting in the round. This means you would start this particular skirt with 200 stitches.

HEM TO HIP: Using a circular needle, cast on 200 stitches. Join, making sure all your stitches are going in the same direction on the needle. Knit 1 row. Check stitches again, making sure the stitches are straight around the needle. (See drawing at Circular Needles under NEE- DLES; it shows stitches in the proper direction.) Decide what kind of a hem to make (see HEMS).

Now, let us decide how to decrease the skirt to fit at the hip. Starting with 200 stitches for the hem and needing 152 stitches at the hip (38 inches times 4 stitches), we find that we have 48 stitch- es to lose between the hem and the hip. (This can safely be rounded to 50 stitches to make the calculations that follow easier.)

The length of the skirt between the hem and the hip depends on the length of leg between hip and knee and the desired length of the skirt below the knee. Let us assume the skirt is to be 28 inches long. Allowing 9 inches from waist to hip, plus a 1-inch stretch in blocking, the length of the skirt from hip to bottom will be 18 inches.

Your object is to shape the skirt, grad- ually decreasing from the hem to the hip. A desirable number of stitches to decrease in one row is 10 stitches. This number does not depend on gauge, the number of stitches to the inch; it just simplifies the decreasing calculations. For this example, decreasing (losing) 50 stitches at the rate of 10 stitches per decrease row means making 5 decrease rows. We now see that we have an 18 inch length in which to lose 50 stitches in 5 decrease rows, losing 10 stitches in each decrease row.

To shape a straight skirt properly so that there is a gradual decrease from the hem to the hip, the decreases are usually made approximately every 2 inches. It is advisable to work at least 5 or 6 inches before starting to decrease on a straight skirt. So the decrease rows for our exam- ple will fall within 13 inches (18 inches from hip to hem minus 5 inches for getting to the starting point). Divide 13 by 5 (the number of decrease rows). This gives approximately 2½, so we will work 2½ inches between each decrease row and after the last one. Now we know the decreasing will be accomplished over 12½ inches, which tells us that we need to knit 5½ inches before making the first decrease (5½ plus 12½ totals 18, the length from the hem to the hip).

Mark the beginning of the first row with a ring marker or piece of yarn, so that the decreases fall above each other in the decrease rows. To decrease 10 stitches in one row of 200 stitches, *knit 18 stitches, knit 2 together* repeating the directions between the asterisks across the row. This leaves 190 stitches to work for 2½ inches. The next decrease will be *knit 17 stitches, knit 2 together* across the row (180 stitches left).

Continue making the decreases by knitting 1 less stitch between the decreases on the decrease row. For the example we are using, follow these directions:

1. Knit 2½ inches. *Knit 16, knit 2 together* (170 stitches left).
2. Knit 2½ inches. *Knit 15, knit 2 together* (160 stitches left).
3. Knit 2½ inches. *Knit 14, knit 2 together* (150 stitches left).
4. Knit 2½ inches.

HIP TO WAIST: You are now ready to start decreasing to the waist. Your waist measurement for our example is 26 inches. To find the number of stitches needed for the waist, multiply 26 inches times 4 stitches to the inch. This equals 104 stitches. You must allow room for the skirt to go over your shoulders or hips. Therefore, add at least 1½ inches (6 stitches) to this measurement. This means we need 110 stitches at the waist for our example. We have 9 inches (the measurement from the hip to the waist) in which to decrease 40 stitches. One inch of the 9 inches goes toward making the waistband. You are left with 8 inches in which to lose 40 stitches at the rate of 10 stitches in each decrease row. This means you will have 4 decrease rows. To find out how far apart to make these decrease rows, divide 8 inches by 4 rows. Therefore, make these decreases every 2 inches 4 times.

WAISTBAND: Work straight until 28 inches from the start of the skirt. Cast off the 110 stitches very loosely. (The best way to do this is to cast off using a needle a couple of sizes larger than the one you have been using for knitting.)

Do not break the yarn when you get to your last stitch. Instead, return to your regular-size needle and begin the waistband by picking up a stitch in the front half of each cast-off stitch until you have 110 stitches back on your needle. Knit ¾ inch. Then purl 1 row. Knit 1 row less than ¾ inch and cast off loosely (again using the larger needle). This is the waistband.

Break the yarn about 1 yard from the last stitch. Then fold the waistband on the purl row and weave to the cast-off stitches of the skirt, leaving a ½-inch opening to run elastic through.

There are other ways to make waistbands. See WAISTBANDS.

A-Line Skirt

An A-line skirt falls away from the body from the hip down, but it does not flare out. To get the A-line to fall properly, decrease in gores or lines as in the drawing. You can make your skirt with 4 gores, 6 gores, 8 gores, or more.

A-line skirt

For the purposes of illustration, we will do a 4-gore skirt. The width at the hem of an A-line skirt is at least 18 inches wider than the hip measurement. Take the hip and waist measurement (see MEASURING THE BODY) and decide on the length you want for the skirt. For this example, we will assume that the hip measurement is 38 inches. With a hip measurement of 38 inches and 18 inches for the width of the hem, you need 56 inches at the bottom of the skirt. Determine the number of stitches to the inch for the yarn you are using (see GAUGE). Multiply the number of stitches to the inch by the width at the bottom of the skirt. For this example we are using a gauge of 4 stitches to the inch. Cast on 224 stitches for the bottom of the skirt (56 inches times 4 stitches to the inch).

With 224 stitches at the hem and 152 stitches (38 inches times 4 stitches to the inch) needed at the hip, you have 72 stitches to lose. Making 4 gores means you are decreasing at 4 points equally divided around the skirt. You will decrease 2 stitches only at each of these points, or a total of 8 stitches in each decrease row.

To make sure that you always decrease in the same place to form the gore line, divide the number of stitches by 4 and place a marker at each dividing point. In this example, place a marker at the beginning, where you joined the row, and after each section of 56 stitches. Decrease 1 stitch before and after each marker, starting the first decrease after the marker.

The decreases are done as follows: At the beginning of the row, knit the first 2 stitches after the marker together; work up to the last 2 stitches before the next marker; slip 1 stitch, knit the next stitch, pass the slip stitch over the knit stitch; slip the marker; knit 2 stitches together. Repeat these decreases before and after the other markers up to the last 2 stitches in the row. Then slip 1 stitch, knit 1 stitch, pass slip stitch over the knit stitch. The reason for starting the row with a decrease *after* the marker, then decreasing before and after the next 3 markers, and finally decreasing the last 2 stitches in the row is to make the first and last decreases come out on the same row.

This decreases 8 stitches in one row. Let us assume that the length of the skirt from the hip down is 18 inches. There are 72 stitches to be decreased. Divide 72 stitches (the number to be decreased) by 8 stitches (the number you are decreasing in one row). You will have to make your row of decreases every 2 inches, 9 times.

An A-line skirt is made the same from the hips to the waist as is a straight skirt. You have 9 inches in which to decrease 40 stitches. Subtract 1 inch for the waistband. This leaves 40 stitches to be decreased in 8 inches, decreasing 8 stitches each decrease row. Continue to decrease every 1½ inches 5 times. Work even until the skirt is 28 inches. Cast off loosely. Do not break the yarn. Pick up for waistband (see under Straight Skirt or in WAISTBAND section).

Flared Skirt

A flared skirt swings out from the hips in a circular fashion. When making a flared skirt, your first decision is how wide you want the skirt to be at the hem, or how much of a flare you want. A very full flared skirt measures 120 inches at the hem, but a flare can be as small as 86 inches at the hem.

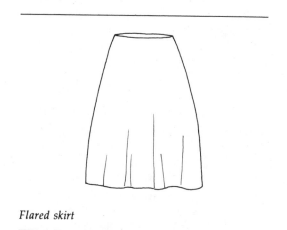

Flared skirt

Determine the number of stitches to the inch for the yarn and needles you plan to use (see GAUGE). For our example we will assume that your gauge is 7 stitches to 2 inches (3½ stitches to the inch) and 8 rows to 2 inches and that you prefer a smaller flare of 92 inches at the hem. Multiplying the number of stitches to the inch by the number of inches needed gives 322 stitches. To make the calculations for decreasing simpler, round this number to 325 stitch-es and cast onto circular needles. We will also assume that the waist on the finished skirt is to be 26 inches, allowing 2 inches for stretch so that you can easily pull the skirt over your shoulders or put on over your hips. With a measurement of 26 inches at the waist you will need 91 stitches there (3½ stitches to the inch times 26 inches). For ease in calculating, round this number to 90 stitches.

Since we are starting out with 325 stitches at the hem and need to finish with 90 stitches at the waist, we need to lose, or decrease, 235 stitches. The length of the skirt for our example is 28 inches. Subtracting 1 inch for the waistband means that we need to decrease these stitches within 27 inches. To give the flare effect, most of the decreasing is done up to the middle of the skirt; the rest of the decreasing needed is worked in more gradually. For this example, decrease 25 stitches evenly across the row every 2½ inches 8 times (a total of 200 stitches decreased). Decrease the remaining 35 stitches by decreasing 5 stitches evenly across the row every inch. Finish with a WAISTBAND.

Dirndl Skirt

Here are two ways of making a skirt with a gathered waist.

METHOD 1: This skirt works best when made of a fine yarn, such as sports-weight yarn. It is worked straight from the hip to the waist with no decreasing for shaping. (Skirts made this way of heavier yarn will be too bulky at the waist. If you are plann~ ~irndl skirt of heavier yarn, ~ou.)   ~d meth~d~

Dirndl skirt

To make the skirt, follow directions for the straight skirt as given, up to the hip. Do not make any decreases. Knit straight to the waist. Purl 1 row, work 1 inch more, cast off loosely. Fold top of skirt back at purl row. Sew down edge to purl side, leaving ½-inch opening. Run a ¾-inch elastic through the band. Adjust the elastic to the waist size, sew the ends together, and sew down the ½-inch open space. For hints about elastic, see WAISTBANDS.

M E T H O D 2: Following instructions for the straight skirt, work up to 1 inch less than the desired length.

Measure your waistline. Add 3 inches to the measurement to allow for stretch so your skirt can be put on easily over the head or the hips. Multiply by the number of stitches you are getting to the inch.

For example, if the waistline measures 29 inches, adding 3 inches gives a total inches. If the number of stitches

you are getting to the inch is 3½, multiplying 32 by 3½ gives the number of stitches you need for the finished waist (112). Let us also assume that you have 168 stitches on your needle. You have 56 stitches to decrease. To do this, decrease the stitches evenly across the row. (If you need help in figuring out how to do this, see DECREASING.) In this example, you would *knit 1 stitch, knit 2 together*, repeating the instructions between asterisks across the row. Cast off the stitches. Add the waistband and run elastic through it. For instructions on how to do this, see WAISTBANDS.

Side-to-Side Knit Skirt (Vertically Knit Skirt)

Make a GAUGE using the garter stitch. Count the number of stitches to the inch and the number of rows to the inch. Take your hip and waist measurements, or the measurements of the person the skirt is intended for (see MEASURING THE BODY), and decide on the finished skirt length.

For this example, assume that your gauge is 7 stitches to 2 inches (3½ stitches to the inch) and 10 rows (5 ridges of garter stitch) to the inch. Also assume a waist of 28 inches, hips of 36 inches, and a skirt length of 27 inches. Subtract 2 inches from the length of the skirt to allow for a 2-inch finishing border, and subtract 1 inch from the length of the skirt to allow for the waistband. (If you prefer a smaller border, make the proper adjustment in these subtractions.) If you are knitting with wool or other natural yarn, subtract 1 inch from the length of the skirt to allow for stretching when

Skirt knit from side to side

blocking. (If you are knitting with synthetic yarn, do not make this last deduction.) The body of the skirt is now 23 inches in length.

Add 18 inches to the hip measurement for the width at the bottom of the skirt. The measurements now are: 28 inches for the waist, 36 inches for the hips, and 54 inches for the bottom of the skirt. With a gauge of 3½ stitches to the inch and a length of 23 inches, calculate the number of stitches you need for the length. Do this by multiplying 23 times 3½ stitches to the inch. This equals 80½ stitches. Since you cannot cast on half a stitch, work with 81 stitches.

Always remember you are not working this skirt round. You are working the skirt vertically, in 6 panels.

Gradual shaping is needed to give the skirt a proper line, and the skirt will fall better if the wide part of the skirt at the bottom is 5 inches deep.

CASTING ON THE FIRST PANEL: Cast on 18 stitches (or the number of stitches according to your gauge that will make 5 inches).

ROW 1: Knit.
ROW 2: Knit. Add on 11 stitches (or the number of stitches you need to make 3 inches). For directions for adding on stitches see ADDING ON STITCHES. You now have 29 stitches.
ROW 3: Turn. Slip the first stitch, knit to the end of the row. Turn.
ROW 4: Knit back. Add on 10 stitches (39 stitches).
ROW 5: Slip the first stitch. Knit to the end of the row. Turn.
ROW 6: Knit back. Add on 11 stitches (50 stitches).
ROW 7: Slip the first stitch. Knit to the end of the row. Turn.
ROW 8: Knit back. Add on 10 stitches (60 stitches).
ROW 9: Slip the first stitch. Knit to the end of the row. Turn.
ROW 10: Knit back. Add on 11 stitches (71 stitches).
ROW 11: Slip the first stitch. Knit to the end of the row. Turn.
ROW 12: Knit back. Add on 10 stitches.
ROW 13: Slip the first stitch. Knit to the end of the row. Turn.
ROW 14: Knit the row back.

You now have 81 stitches (the length of the skirt).

This skirt is made in 6 panels. Therefore, the top of each panel for a 28-inch waistline should be 4⅔ inches. Since the garter stitch is stretchy, allow just 4½ inches for the top of each panel. The gauge is 10 rows to the inch (or 5 ridges of garter stitch—it is easier to count ridges). You need 45 rows or 23 ridges to make the top of the panel 4½ inches wide.

WORKING THE FIRST PANEL: Work 45 rows (23 ridges) on the 81 stitches, ending with the yarn at the top part of the panel (the narrower part).

ROW 1: Cast off 10 stitches very loosely. Knit the rest of the row.

ROW 2: Knit back.

ROW 3: Cast off 11 stitches. Start the casting off by slipping the first stitch. Finish the row.

ROW 4: Knit back.

ROW 5: Cast off 10 stitches, slipping the first stitch. Knit the rest of the row.

ROW 6: Knit back.

ROW 7: Cast off 11 stitches, slipping the first stitch. Knit the rest of the row.

ROW 8: Knit back.

ROW 9: Cast off 10 stitches, slipping the first stitch. Knit the rest of the row.

ROW 10: Knit back.

ROW 11: Cast off 11 stitches, slipping the first stitch. Knit the rest of the row.

ROW 12: Knit back.

ROW 13: Cast off the remaining stitches, slipping the first stitch.

Do not break the yarn. Leave the last stitch on the needle.

PICKING UP THE SECOND PANEL:

Turn and pick up stitches for the next panel, as follows:

ROW 1: Pick up the 17 stitches you just cast off (with the stitch left on the needle, you have 18 stitches).

ROW 2: Turn. Slip the first stitch, knit the rest of the row.

ROW 3: Turn. Knit back. Pick up the next 11 stitches that were cast off (you now have 29 stitches).

ROW 4: Turn. Slip the first stitch, knit the rest of the row.

ROW 5: Turn. Knit back. Pick up the next 10 stitches that were cast off (39 stitches).

ROW 6: Turn. Slip the first stitch, knit the rest of the row.

ROW 7: Turn. Knit back. Pick up the next 11 stitches that were cast off (50 stitches).

ROW 8: Turn. Slip the first stitch. Knit the rest of the row.

ROW 9: Turn. Knit back. Pick up the next 10 stitches that were cast off (60 stitches).

ROW 10: Turn. Slip the first stitch. Knit the rest of the row.

ROW 11: Turn. Knit back. Pick up the next 11 stitches that were cast off (71 stitches).

ROW 12: Turn. Slip the first stitch. Knit the rest of the row.

ROW 13: Turn. Knit back. Pick up the last 10 stitches that were cast off (81 stitches).

WORKING THE OTHER PANELS: You are now ready to work your second panel. Go back to the instructions for working the first panel and repeat from that point until you have 6 panels. Cast off the last panel the same as the others (first 10 stitches, then 11 stitches, 10 stitches, 11 stitches, 10 stitches, 11 stitches, 18 stitches). Finish off the last stitch, leaving an end of yarn long enough to weave the first and last panel together. Weave the seam, starting at the bottom of the skirt (see WEAVING).

WAISTBAND: The skirt will look much too wide at the top. Don't worry. Connect the yarn to the top of the skirt at the point where you finished your seam. Pick up 20 stitches across each panel (120 stitches). For the waistband, work 1 inch in stockinette stitch, ending with a knit row. Purl 1 row. Work 1 row less than 1 inch. Cast off loosely. Fold back with the purl row at the top and sew to the row where the stitches were picked up, leaving the last ½ inch undone. Run elastic through the waistband and then sew down the ½-inch opening.

BORDER: Make a 2-inch bottom border following any of the instructions given under Unstructured Hems in the HEMS section.

Sleeveless Sweaters and Dresses

When making a sleeveless sweater or dress, plan the armhole 1 inch longer than the armhole you would make for a sweater with sleeves. For a sleeveless sweater, follow the instructions for Classic Round-neck Sweater under SWEATERS, making this adjustment in the armhole. See DRESSES for general directions about dresses.

Finish off the sleeveless armhole so that it fits snugly at the top of the arm and does not gap. Armholes can be finished simply by crocheting around them in a single crochet, a slip stitch, or a combination of both stitches. Or stitches can be picked up from the armhole edge and knitted into a band of single or double thickness. The band can be made in ribbing, in the garter stitch, or in the stockinette stitch.

Knitted Armhole Band

For a knitted armhole band, first determine the size of the armhole on the finished sweater or dress. Do not stretch the armhole when measuring. Lay the garment flat and measure the armhole straight up from the first decrease row to the first cast-off stitch on the shoulder (see MEASURING KNITTING).

The best way to prepare your garment so you can easily make a knitted armhole band is to sew the sides of the sleeveless top but leave the shoulder seams unsewn. Finish the armhole bands before finishing the neck or neck bands.

To figure out how many stitches to pick up for the front part of a knitted armhole band, multiply the number of stitches to the inch in your gauge for the yarn you are using by the number of inches in the armhole measurement you just made. You can use a circular needle a size smaller than was used to knit the garment and knit back and forth on it.

With the right side of the front of the garment facing you and starting at the right shoulder, pick up the required number of stitches along the front part of the armhole up to the cast-off stitches at the bottom of the armhole. Pick up a stitch in each of the cast-off stitches at the underarm, and then pick up the same number of stitches for the back part of the armhole as you picked up in the front. Place a marker in the middle of the row of picked-up stitches. This marks the center of the underarm. You will shape the armhole band at the underarm.

Ribbed Armhole Band Work as follows on the picked-up stitches: Knit 1, purl 1 up to 2 stitches before the marker. Slip 1, knit 1, pass the slip stitch over the knit stitch. Slip the marker from the left-hand needle to the right-hand needle. Knit 2 stitches together. Finish the row with knit 1, purl 1. Work in this ribbing, repeating the decreases before and after the marker every row, until the armhole band is almost 1 inch wide. Cast off loosely. Sew shoulder seams (see Shoulder Seams under WEAVING), including the 1-inch opening at the top of the armhole band.

Double Armhole Band Work on the picked-up stitches in a stockinette stitch for ¾ inch, decreasing 2 stitches each row, one on either side of the marker. Purl 1 row on the knit side. Then work in knitting for 1 row less than you did for the outside of the band, at the same time increasing 1 stitch every row on either side of the marker. Cast off loose-ly. Sew shoulder seams, including opening in band. Fold band back on purl row and sew into place with yarn on the wrong side of the neck.

Crocheted Armhole Band

Before making a crocheted band, sew the shoulder seams. Starting at the top of the armhole, with the right side facing you, do a row of single crochet around the armhole. Make sure that each stitch is made in the little nub at the edge of the armhole. You might need to do an occasional stitch between the nubs to keep the armhole lying flat. Turn and finish with a row of slip stitch, making a slip stitch in each single crochet. Do this row loosely.

Sleeves

There are many ways to make a sleeve, and I have explained some of them elsewhere in this book. To make a raglan, see RAGLAN SLEEVE. To make a set-in sleeve, see the directions for Sleeve under the Classic Round-neck Sweater section of SWEATERS. You can make a sleeve as part of a sweater by starting at the wrist, knitting up the sleeve, and then working vertically across the sweater, finishing with the other sleeve. This kind of sleeve, which has no shoulder definition, can be found under Side-to-Side Knit Sweater in the SWEATERS section of this book. For a sleeve made to go with a drop shoulder, see DROP

SHOULDER. To match stripes in a sleeve to the body of a sweater that also has stripes, see STRIPES.

Remember to measure the length of the arm accurately before knitting the sleeve. Take this measurement from a point 1 inch below the armpit to the wrist.

Slip Stitches

Knit Slip Stitch

A slip stitch in knitting is a stitch that is slipped from one needle to another without being knitted. When slipping a stitch from one needle to another as part of the decrease for shaping, slip the stitch as if you were going to knit. When working a pattern that calls for a slip stitch, unless the instructions tell you otherwise, slip the stitch as if you were going to purl.

Crochet slip stitch

Crochet Slip Stitch

The crochet slip stitch is included in this book about knitting because it is frequently used to finish edges. To do a crochet slip stitch, connect the yarn into the end stitch when you have an edge, or into the first cast-on stitch when you have a piece worked in the round. Place the crochet hook back into the same space where the yarn is connected. Hook the yarn over the crochet hook and pull it through the space and the stitch on the crochet hook. If you are slip-stitching along a purl row, place the crochet hook in the loop of the purl stitch. If you are slip-stitching across rows of garter stitch or stockinette stitch (such as you might have on the front edge of a cardigan sweater), place the crochet hook into the nub at the end of the row. Draw the yarn through, making a second loop on the crochet hook and then drawing this second loop through the first loop on the crochet hook, loosely. Go into the next stitch or nub and loosely pull this loop through the loop in the needle. Continue in this manner until you have worked a slip stitch to the end of the edge. Pull yarn through last loop. Break yarn. Work in end on wrong side (see FINISHING).

As you work, observe the edge you are adding the slip stitch to. If you are working the slip stitch too loosely, the stitches will gap and the edge will not lie flat. If you work your slip stitch too tightly, the edge will draw in and the knitted piece will not fall properly. If you observe either of these problems, rip the slip stitches back to the beginning and begin again, adjusting your tension. If your stitches are still coming out too loose, try skipping an occasional stitch when you work with the crochet hook. Usually skipping every fifth stitch will do the trick, but you will have to experiment with your edge and needle.

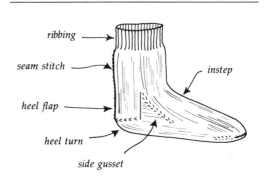

Sock

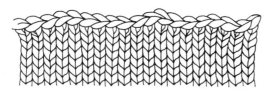

Slip stitch worked too loose

Slip stitch worked too tight

Socks

Socks are not difficult to make. They just take patience . . . at least the first one does. The second gives you a little more confidence. Then, when you feel at ease

making them, you can settle into your most comfortable chair and enjoy yourself.

Here is a guide to sock length. But remember this is only a guide. You must use your judgment. Not everyone wants a sock to end at the same point. And one length will fall in a different place on a short, stocky leg than on a long, slim leg. Make the sock to fit the wearer.

First measure the foot from the toe to the heel. For knee socks, the leg length is 2 times the length of the foot. For half socks, the leg length equals the length of the foot. For ankle socks, the leg length is half the length of the foot. None of these measurements includes the ribbing at the top of the sock.

All socks need ribbing at the top to guarantee a more snug fit. This applies even when making a fancy top or cuff to the sock.

If your sock is to have a cuff, remember that when you finish working the cuff, you must turn it inside out before starting to work the sock. This brings the right side of the cuff, when turned, to the right side of the sock.

A good gauge to follow for socks is 9 stitches to 2 inches (4½ stitches to the inch). You can achieve this gauge using a heavy sport yarn or knitting worsted. Use needles that give you this gauge. Try needles size 4, 5, or 6, depending on how tightly or loosely you knit.

Knee Socks

The number of stitches cast on should be enough to fit around the ankle. We will work on 64 stitches for the top of the sock here and will knit with 4 double-pointed needles.

RIBBING: Cast the 64 stitches on one of the double-pointed needles. Let the end of the yarn hang to define the beginning of the row, or place a marker at this point. With the first needle, knit 1, purl 1 for 12 stitches. Pick up the second needle and knit 1, purl 1 for 20 stitches, making sure to pull the yarn when working the first two stitches on the second needle so there is no space between the ribbing. Pick up the third needle and knit 1, purl 1 for 20 stitches, again making sure to pull the yarn when doing the first two stitches. Slip the last 12 stitches onto the first needle and knit 1, purl 1 across these stitches. Slip marker to the right-hand needle. Then continue knitting in ribbing across the first needle with the fourth needle, so that there are 24 stitches on this needle. Make sure to move the marker from one needle to the other. Don't forget that the marker designates the end of one row and the beginning of the next row.

Using your free needle, knit the stitches in ribbing off the next needle. Take the free needle and knit the stitches in ribbing off the next needle. Continue in this manner for 1½ or 2 inches, ending at the marker. Add 1 stitch to the needle by picking up 1 stitch from the back of the last needle. This is the seam stitch.

LEG: Knit around, switching from ribbing to all knit stitches. Knit for 1 inch. To shape the leg part of the sock, you first increase for the part that goes over the calf and then decrease as you knit toward the ankle. Consider the width of the calf that the sock is intended for. If you are making the sock for a very slim leg, it is not necessary to make any increases here. If the leg and ankle are heavy, decrease only 2 times for the shaping instead of the 4 times recommended in the sample instructions that follow.

Increase 1 stitch after the seam stitch and knit around to 1 stitch before the seam stitch. Increase this stitch and knit the seam stitch. This keeps the increases in the same row. Work 1 inch. Increase the same way around a second time.

Then decrease as follows: Knit the seam stitch. Slip 1 stitch, knit 1 stitch, pass the slip stitch over the knit stitch. Knit around until you reach the 2 stitches before the seam stitch; knit these 2 stitches together. Work 1 inch. Decrease 3 more times in the same manner, knitting 1 inch between each decrease row (you will have 20 stitches on the needle).

Now knit straight to the ankle.

HEEL: Half the number of stitches on the needles will be used to make the heel. To make it easier to knit the heel, shift (not knit) the stitches so that half of them are on one needle: Instead of 61 stitches on 3 needles, put 31 on one needle to be worked for the heel. The center stitch of these 31 stitches must be the seam stitch.

In shifting the stitches, you may discover that the yarn is hanging loosely in the middle of the needle containing the heel stitches. To correct this, take your free needle, slip the unworked stitches to it, and knit them back onto the heel needle.

Divide the remaining 30 stitches between 2 needles. These stitches will be worked for the instep.

Take the heel needle and turn it so the purl side is facing you. Slip the first stitch, purl 14, knit the seam stitch, purl the last 15 stitches.

Now you have a choice. You can knit the heel in the stockinette stitch or in the heel stitch. The heel stitch, which makes a stronger heel, is worked as follows:

ROW 1: Knit 1, slip 1.
ROW 2: Knit.
ROW 3: Slip 1, knit 1.
ROW 4: Knit.

Repeat these four rows until you have knitted a square piece; that is, the piece you have knitted is as long as it is wide. You can best measure this by lifting the right-hand corner of the piece and bringing it over to the left side. When the flap

is as long as it is wide, you are ready to turn the heel.

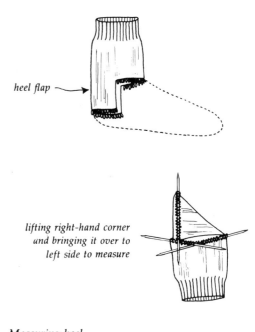

heel flap —

lifting right-hand corner and bringing it over to left side to measure

Measuring heel

In order to turn the heel, you decrease on either side of the seam stitch, making the decreases from the center outward, as follows:

1. Knit 15 stitches. Purl the seam stitch. Knit the next two stitches, then slip 1 stitch, knit 1 stitch, pass

the slip stitch over the knit stitch. Turn.

2. Slip the first stitch. Purl 7, purl 2 stitches together, purl 1. Turn.
3. Slip 1 stitch, knit 8, slip 1 stitch, knit 1 stitch, pass the slip stitch over the knit stitch. Turn.
4. Slip 1, purl 9, purl 2 together, purl 1. Turn.
5. Slip 1, knit 10, slip 1, knit 1, pass the slip stitch over the knit stitch.

Continue working back and forth over the center stitches, always slipping the first stitch, working across, slipping the next to last stitch of the center stitches on the knit row, knitting the next stitch and passing the slip stitch over the knit stitch. Turn. Slip the first stitch on the purl row, purl up to the last stitch of the center stitches and then purl this stitch together with the next purl stitch on the row, followed by a purl stitch. Repeat these 2 rows until all the stitches are back on the needles. Finish on the purl side.

SIDE GUSSETS: Knit across the needle. You now have one side of the heel between your needle and the next needle. With the needle holding the stitches for the heel, pick up and knit 1 stitch in each loop along the side, picking up the inside of the stitch. Knit 3 stitches from the first needle holding the instep stitches. With the free needle, knit the remaining 12 stitches from the first instep needle and the first 12 stitches from the next instep needle. With the free needle, knit the last 3 stitches off this needle; then pick up and knit the same number

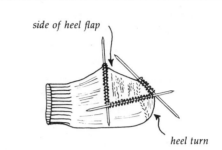

Picking up stitches along the side of the heel flap for side gusset

of stitches you picked up along the other side of the flap. Continue knitting with this needle across the heel up to the seam stitch. Knit the next row. On the instep needles, decrease as follows:

ROUND 1: Knit up to the last 5 stitches, knit 2 stitches together, knit 3. Knit across the next needle. (This is the heel needle.) On the next needle knit 3, slip 1 stitch, knit 1 stitch, pass the slip stitch over the knit stitch. Knit the rest of the round.
ROUND 2: Knit around on all needles.

Repeat these two rounds until 17 stitches remain on each of the two needles being decreased. Knit the first 14 stitches from the heel needle to the left of the instep needle. With free needle, knit the next 3 stitches off this needle. Knit across the

24 stitches on the next needle and then knit the first 3 stitches from the beginning of the third needle. With free needle, knit the last 14 stitches from the last needle. The two needles with the 14 stitches each hold the stitches for the sole of the sock. The needle with the 30 stitches holds the stitches for the instep.

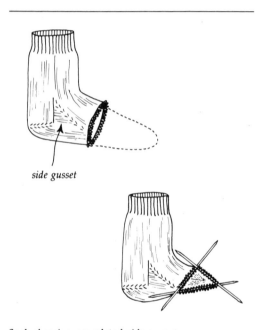

side gusset

Sock showing completed side gusset

FOOT: Knit even until 1 inch less than length of foot. The sole of the sock is knit in the stockinette stitch. The instep can be continued in pattern if one is being used for the sock.

TOE: Shift the stitches so that the instep needle has the same number of stitches as the two needles with the stitches for the sole. If there is one extra stitch on the sole side, knit 2 stitches together at the end of the first needle (at the center of the sole). Decrease for the toe as follows:

> **ROUND 1**: Knit up to last 3 stitches of first needle, knit 2 stitches together, knit 1. On the second needle (instep stitches), knit 1 stitch, slip 1 stitch, knit 1 stitch, pass the slip stitch over the knit stitch; knit to last 3 stitches, knit 2 stitches together, knit 1. On the third needle, knit 1, slip 1, knit 1, pass the slip stitch over the knit stitch; knit to the end of needle.
>
> **ROUND 2**: Knit.

Repeat these 2 rounds until there are 2 stitches on the first needle, 4 stitches on the second needle, and 2 stitches on the third needle. Slip the 2 stitches from the first and third needle together so they are all on one needle.

FINISHING: There are many ways to finish off the toe. Here are three. The simplest method is the first.

1. Knit the first stitch on one needle together with the first stitch on the other needle. Repeat for the second stitch on each needle. Cast off by pulling the first stitch over the sec-

ond. Repeat for the rest of the stitches.

2. Cast off the 8 stitches. Weave together.
3. Graft the stitches together (see GRAFTING).

Ankle Socks

Follow the directions already given for socks. Make a 2-inch ribbed top on needles one size smaller than you will use for the rest of the sock. Decide on the length of the ankle part and work this part in a stockinette stitch or pattern stitch on the needles used to work the gauge, making no increases or decreases. Continue following directions for the heel, side gussets, foot, and toe.

Half Socks

The length of the top of half socks is usually the same as the foot length. Take these measurements and follow the directions already given for socks. Half socks usually have a 2-inch ribbed top, knitted on needles one size smaller than those you plan to use for the socks themselves.

band you will pick up). Let us assume that you have 56 stitches on your needle at this point. To figure out how many stitches you will use for the square neck, you must first know how many stitches you need for the shoulders and subtract 1 inch to allow for the band you will pick up. Shoulder seams are usually 4 inches; subtracting 1 inch for the band border, and using a gauge of 4 stitches to the inch, you need 12 stitches for each shoulder, or a total of 24. Subtracting these 24 stitches from the 56 on your needle leaves 32 stitches, the number you will use to make a square neck.

Sweater with square neckline

Square Neckline

Decide how deep you want your square neckline to be and work up the front of the garment to 1 inch less than the depth you have chosen (to allow for the

Place these center 32 stitches on a stitch holder. Work up each shoulder section until it is the same depth as the back to the top of the shoulder. Cast off the shoulder stitches going from the armhole side to the neck by casting off 6 stitches 2 times. Weave the shoulder seams to-

gether (see Shoulder Seams under WEAV-
ING).

Worked in the Round

Using a circular needle one size smaller
than you used to knit the garment, connect the yarn at the back of the neck on
the right-hand side. Knit across the
stitches for the back. Then pick up 1
stitch for each nub down the left neck
side, plus 1 extra stitch for every inch.
Knit across the stitches on the stitch
holder at the center front and pick up
the same number of stitches on the right
neck side that you picked up on the left.
Join. Place a marker at each of the four
corners.

Garter-stitch Band

ROW 1: Knit 2 stitches together after
the first marker. Make this
decrease through the back of
the stitches. Knit across the
row to 2 stitches before the
next marker. Knit these 2
stitches together. Repeat this
procedure after and before the
markers for the rest of the
row.

ROW 2: Purl.

Repeat these 2 rows until the border is
the desired depth, usually 1 inch. Cast
off loosely.

Ribbed Band Following the decreases
as described under the garter-stitch band,
work in a ribbing of knit 1, purl 1 for
Rows 1 and 2, instead of knitting the
first row and purling the second. Repeat
the ribbing for 1 inch. Cast off loosely.

Stockinette Band with a Fold-back Facing

1. Decrease after and before the markers the same way as described under
   the garter-stitch band but work in
   the stockinette stitch (all rows knit).
   Work for desired depth.
2. Work 1 row of purl. This is the row
   on which the band will be folded.
3. On the next row, increase the first
   stitch after the marker. Knit across
   to the last stitch before the next
   marker and increase this stitch. Repeat, increasing after and before the
   markers for the rest of the row.
4. Knit around.
5. Repeat the last 2 rows until you
   have 1 row less than the number of
   rows in the border up to the purl
   row. Cast off loosely. Fold back on
   the purl row and sew the fold-back
   part in place.

Worked in Sections

If you prefer not to work the square
neck finishing in the round, you can
work each section separately. Transfer
the stitches from the front stitch holder
to a straight needle a size smaller than
the size you used for the sweater. Work
up in garter stitch, ribbing, or stockinette
stitch for desired depth. Cast off. Sew to
the sides of the neck. Then pick up the
stitches from the back and work the
same. Sew to the sides of the neck. Then
pick up 1 stitch in each nub on one side
of the neck plus 1 extra stitch for each
inch. Work in the same stitch for the
same number of rows as before. Cast off.

Repeat on the other side of the neck. Sew the sides down.

Stitches

Here are the directions for making the basic stitches of knitting, after the knit stitch and the purl stitch, which are explained under KNITTING. You can also find directions for other stitches in this book. A variety of cable stitches is included under CABLES. See HATS for a group of stretchy stitches and ARAN KNITTING for directions for many of the pattern stitches used in this beautiful knitting. For a stitch of double thickness that you might want to use for making coats or jackets, see DOUBLE KNITTING. For a dropped stitch that creates an openwork pattern, see DROPPED STITCH. And for some stitches to work at edges, see SELVEDGE STITCHES.

Many of the pattern stitches described here are based on a multiple of a certain number of stitches (see Multiple of Stitches under INSTRUCTIONS). In order for these pattern stitches to work, the multiple of stitches specified must not be changed.

Remember: When making a gauge swatch, make the swatch using the pattern stitch.

Stockinette Stitch   The stockinette stitch is the one you usually think of when you visualize knitting. It is a simple stitch to make and can be used on all garments where a flat stockinglike surface is desired. You can use any type of yarn to make this stitch, selecting the needles you use to knit the yarn so that the stitch has the closeness you want. To make a stockinette stitch using two needles, knit across the first row and purl back; repeat these 2 rows. When working in the round, knit all the rows.

Garter Stitch   The garter stitch produces a knitted piece that has a ribbed effect. It looks the same on both sides, so it is reversible. It can be used for borders on sweaters, jackets, coats, or any other part of a garment where borders are appropriate. It can also be used as the main stitch for a sweater, jacket, hat, or scarf as well as for an afghan or blanket. The garter stitch is particularly effective when used in garments that are knitted from side to side, or vertically, instead of horizontally.

The garter stitch has more stretch to it than the stockinette stitch. Allow for the fact that garments made of the garter stitch will stretch more in blocking.

To make the garter stitch when using straight needles, knit every row. To make the garter stitch in the round (with circular needles), knit the first row, purl the second row, and repeat these 2 rows.

Always make a gauge before starting your garment. This is one stitch I would suggest blocking before measuring your gauge.

Ribbing   Most sweaters and some skirts and jackets begin with ribbing. Ribbing is also used as a pattern stitch for a garment. For the border on a sweater, use a needle one size smaller on the ribbing if you want to hold the waist-band in and give the sweater shape. If you want the sweater to be straight, use the same size needle for the ribbing as for the rest of your garment.

Ribbing on an Even Number of Stitches

ROW 1: Knit 1, purl 1.
ROW 2: Knit 1, purl 1.
Repeat these two rows for pattern.

Ribbing on an Odd Number of Stitches

ROW 1: Knit 1, purl 1.
ROW 2: Purl 1, knit 1.
Repeat these two rows for pattern.

Wider Ribbing   (multiple of 4)

ROW 1: Knit 2, purl 2.
ROW 2: Knit 2, purl 2.
Repeat these two rows for pattern.

Wider Ribbing   (multiple of 4 + 2)

ROW 1: Knit 2, purl 2.
ROW 2: Purl 2, knit 2.
Repeat these two rows for pattern.

Wider Knit Rib   Ribbing also can be done in a variety of patterns. For instance, if you want a wider knit rib, work purl 2, knit 3.

Yarn Over

This stitch creates a hole and is used to make buttonholes or is worked as part of lacy patterns. It adds an extra stitch to the row. Yarn-over stitches are usually worked on the knit side, although you can make one on the purl side if your instructions call for it.

When making a yarn over on the knit side, bring the yarn from the back and place it between the two needles so that the end is toward you. Then put the yarn over the right-hand needle in a direction going away from you. Work the next stitch.

Yarn-over stitch

The yarn over adds 1 stitch. You will usually find that your instructions tell you on a subsequent row to knit 2 stitches together. This eliminates the added yarn-over stitch.

Continental or Twisted Stitch

This stitch gives more body to the yarn you are working with but makes a flat surface. When this stitch is used, the knitted piece looks as if it had been woven instead of knitted.

ROW 1: Knit each stitch working across the row, through the back of the stitch.

ROW 2: When working back and forth on straight or circular needles, purl this row. When working in the round, knit this row.
Repeat these 2 rows for pattern.

Moss Stitch (also called Seed Stitch or Rice Stitch)

This stitch, a beautiful one no matter what it is called, is always worked on an *odd* number of stitches when working back and forth on straight or circular needles, and an *even* number of stitches when working in the round on circular needles. It and the two stitches that follow give a garment a pebbly look. They are all reversible. For an *odd* number of stitches:

ROW 1: Knit 1, purl 1 across the row, ending with a knit stitch. Repeat this row for pattern.

For an *even* number of stitches:

ROUND 1: Knit 1, purl l.
ROUND 2: Purl 1, knit l.
Repeat these 2 rows for pattern.

Double Moss Stitch (also called Double Seed or Double Rice Stitch

This stitch, worked on a multiple of 4 stitches, is worked the same on straight needles as in the round.

ROW 1: Knit 2, purl 2.
ROW 2: Knit 2, purl 2.
ROW 3: Purl 2, knit 2.
ROW 4: Purl 2, knit 2.
Repeat these 4 rows for pattern.

Half Double Moss Stitch (also called Half Double Seed or Half Double Rice Stitch)

This stitch, worked on a multiple of 4 stitches, is worked the same on straight needles as in the round.

ROW 1: Knit.
ROW 2: Knit 2, purl 2.
ROW 3: Knit.
ROW 4: Purl 2, knit 2.
Repeat these 4 rows for pattern.

Garter Ridge Stitch

This stitch can be worked on any number of stitches. When working back and forth, work as follows:

ROW 1: Knit.
ROW 2: Purl.
ROW 3: Knit.
ROW 4: Knit.
Repeat these 4 rows for pattern.

When working in the round on circular needles:

ROUNDS 1, 2, and 3: Knit.
ROUND 4: Purl.
Repeat these 4 rows for pattern.

Basket Stitch

This stitch, worked on a multiple of 8 stitches, is reversible. It is worked the same back and forth on straight needles as it is in the round on circular needles.

ROWS 1, 2, 3, 4: Knit 4, purl 4.
ROWS 5, 6, 7, 8: Purl 4, knit 4.
Repeat these 8 rows for pattern.

Quaker Stitch

This stitch is worked on any number of stitches. For straight needles:

ROW 1: Knit.
ROW 2: Purl.
ROW 3: Knit.
ROW 4: Knit.
ROW 5: Purl.
ROW 6: Knit.
Repeat these 6 rows for pattern.

For circular needles working in the round:

ROUNDS 1, 2, and 3: Knit.
ROUNDS 4, 5, and 6: Purl.

Waffle Stitch

This stitch is worked on a multiple of 3 stitches. On straight needles:

ROW 1: Knit 2, purl 1.
ROW 2: Knit 1, purl 2.
ROW 3: Knit 2, purl 1.
ROW 4: Knit.
Repeat these 4 rows for pattern.

For circular needles working in the round:

ROUNDS 1, 2, and 3: Knit 2, purl 1.
ROUND 4: Purl.
Repeat these 4 rounds for pattern.

Pebble Stitch

This stitch is worked on a multiple of 2 stitches. On straight needles:

ROW 1: Knit.
ROW 2: Purl.
ROW 3: Knit 2 together across row.
ROW 4: *Knit 1, pick up horizontal thread *before* the next stitch and knit the stitch just picked up*. Repeat stitches between asterisks across the row.
Repeat these 4 rows for pattern.

On circular needles working in the round:

ROUNDS 1 and 2: Knit.
ROUND 3: Knit 2 together across the row.
ROUND 4: *Purl 1, pick up the horizontal thread *before* the next stitch and purl the stitch just picked up*. Repeat stitches between asterisks around.
Repeat these 4 rounds for pattern.

Broken Rib Stitch I

This stitch, worked on a multiple of 4 stitches, is reversible. It is worked the same when working back and forth on straight or circular needles as when working in the round on circular needles.

ROWS 1 THROUGH 6: Knit 2, purl 2.
ROWS 7 THROUGH 12: Purl 2, knit 2.
Repeat these 12 rows for pattern.

Broken Rib Stitch II

This stitch is worked on a multiple of 2 stitches. When working back and forth:

ROW 1: Knit 1, purl 1.
ROW 2: Knit 1, purl 1.
ROW 3: *Knit the first stitch from the front, leave on the needle. Knit the same stitch from the back (you have made 2 stitches out of the one knit stitch),

drop from left needle, purl 1*.
Repeat between asterisks
across the row.
ROW 4: Knit 1, purl 1.
Repeat these 4 rows for pattern.

When working in the round on circular
needles:

ROUNDS 1, 2, and 3: Work the same
as when work-
ing back and
forth (above).
ROUND 4: *Knit 2 together, purl 1*.
Repeat across the round.
Repeat these 4 rounds for pattern.

Box or Check Stitch

This stitch is worked on a multiple of 6
stitches. For straight needles:

ROW 1: Purl 2, knit 4.
ROW 2: Purl.
ROW 3: Purl 2, knit 4.
ROW 4: Purl.
ROW 5: Knit 3, *purl 2, knit 4*, end-
ing with purl 2, knit 1.
ROW 6: Purl.
ROW 7: Knit 3, *purl 2, knit 4*, end-
ing with purl 2, knit 1.
ROW 8: Purl.
Repeat these 8 rows for pattern.

Note: On rows 5 and 7 you start with
knit 3 in order to switch the pattern.
Then you repeat the stitches between the
asterisks (purl 2, knit 4) up to the last 3
stitches. Then purl 2, knit 1.

When working in the round on circular needles, follow the same instructions
as for straight needles, but work all the
even rounds knit instead of purl.

Ribbed Garter Stitch

This stitch is worked on any number of
stitches. On straight needles:

ROWS 1 THROUGH 6: Knit.
ROW 7: Purl.
ROW 8: Knit.
Repeat these 8 rows for pattern.

When working in the round on circular
needles:

ROUND 1: Knit.
ROUND 2: Purl.
ROUND 3: Knit.
ROUND 4: Purl.
ROUND 5: Knit.
ROUND 6: Purl.
ROUNDS 7 AND 8: Knit.
Repeat these 8 rounds for pattern.

Double Piqué Stitch

This stitch is worked on a multiple of 2
stitches. On straight needles:

ROW 1: Knit 1, purl 1.
ROW 2: Purl.
ROW 3: Purl 1, knit 1.
ROW 4: Purl.
Repeat these 4 rows for pattern.

When working on circular needles in
the round, follow the instructions for
straight needles, knitting all the even
rows instead of purling.

Remember: You must be careful when
working a pattern to *start* the row with
the stitches given before the asterisk.
Then repeat the stitches shown between
the asterisks up to the last number of
stitches given after the asterisk. If you
have done the pattern correctly, you will

have the same number of stitches left at the end of the row as the pattern calls for. You finish the row using these last stitches.

Stitch Holders

See under EQUIPMENT

Storing Knits

Never put a knitted garment away for a season without either washing or cleaning it first. Sometimes there are spots on a garment that might not be visible to the eye, but moths will find them a beautiful nesting place.

Folding Knits

You can put knits away by just folding them, stacking one garment on top of another. If the label does not say the yarn has been mothproofed, place moth balls or para crystals in the storage area just to be sure. If you prefer, you can also place each garment in a plastic bag to keep it fresh. But do not put anything you've knitted in plastic bags for storage unless the bags have holes punched in them. Yarn has to breathe. In a bag with no holes, moisture will form and the knitted item can develop mildew. If the bag does not have holes in it, poke some in a few places (of course, before you put in your knit). If you prefer, you can wrap the garments in tissue paper before storing.

Hanging Knits

There is a constant debate about this. A garment that is made a bit smaller and blocked out to size can be hung on a hanger. It will not stretch in the hanging. A garment that is made to size or larger and has not been blocked out will have more of a tendency to stretch in the hanging. When you are not sure, I recommend folding for storage.

To hang a knitted garment, use a padded hanger or cover a wire hanger with tissue. If you use a wire hanger, bend the ends down so that they do not pierce the knit.

I have knits that are ten years old that are kept on hangers during the season I am wearing them, and they have not stretched yet. This includes coats and pants. However, I do not recommend hanging jumpsuits on hangers. They are bottom-heavy and might pull out of shape.

Hand knits are very resilient, and those you are wearing constantly do not have to be folded neatly away in a drawer. You can, of course, put your knits away between wearings. Or you can keep them in a basket or on a shelf. As long as the basket or shelf has no nails or snags for the yarn to catch on, you can safely leave them in these storage areas between use and not worry about them.

Stranding

See Vertical Stripes under COLORS, CHANGING

Stripes

Matching Stripes

When making a striped garment that has striped sleeves, make sure the stripes of the sleeves match the stripe of the body, so that the stripe will appear straight across when the garment is worn. To match the stripes you must knit the sleeves and the body of the garment so that the color and width of the stripe at the underarm of the sleeve is the same as the color and width of the stripe at the underarm of the body of the garment. If you are following printed instructions for a sweater or other garment that has stripes, make sure that the directions given will produce matching stripes in the rows up to the cast off-stitches for the underarm.

If your measurements, particularly for arm length, vary from those given in the instructions, do not make your adjustment by adding or subtracting extra rows at the top of the sleeve if this changes the place where the stripe falls in the sleeve. Instead, measure your sleeve length from the underarm to the wrist. From this length, subtract the number of inches you want for the wrist band. Measure your sweater from the underarm down. Let us assume the body of the sweater is 11 inches and your arm is 18 inches long. Figuring backward from the underarm, work out the stripes of the sleeve so that they match those of the body of the sweater. Then continue plotting the stripes, figuring downward, until you arrive at the measurement needed for the sleeve length.

Sewing Striped Garments

When working in stripes, be sure to leave sufficient yarn of the same color hanging free at the beginning of the stripe rows. Use this yarn to weave the stripes together where they meet at the seams.

Making a One-row Stripe

Here is a way to knit a stripe of one row only when working on straight needles. If you use this method you will not have to break the yarn at the end of the row. Knit the one-row stripe using a double-pointed needle or a circular needle the same size as the straight needle you are using for working your garment. Work the row across. Then do not turn the work, as you normally would do, but go back to the start of the row you just finished, pick up the basic color you are working with, and proceed to knit.

Making Stripes of More Than One Row

For information about working with more than one color, see COLORS, CHANGING.

Sweaters

A classic sweater, with a round (crew) neck and set-in sleeves, is the easiest kind to make. It is a basic sweater that should be mastered by all knitters. From the basic sweater, unlimited variations can be developed. The neckline can be changed to a V, a boat, or a square, or a collar can be added. The neckline can be knitted into a turtleneck or a cowl. Or the classic sweater can be extended to a full-length sweater dress.

The sleeves can also be varied. The set-in sleeve usually found in a classic sweater can be changed to a raglan or a full sleeve. Or the sweater can be made sleeveless. The shoulder can be the usual shoulder made by decreasing at the armhole, or it can be changed to a dropped shoulder by knitting straight up from the waist without decreasing for the armhole at all.

The average lengths for a classic pullover, measuring down from the underarm but not including the ribbing, are:

Waist length	9 inches
Top-of-hip length	12 inches
Mid-hip length	16 inches
Dress length	34 inches

Classic Round-neck Sweater

Here are sample instructions for a basic sweater knitted to waist length, with a round (crew) neck, set-in sleeves, and a ribbed band at the bottom.

Straight needles are usually indicated in instructions for sweaters. I prefer using circular needles wherever possible. For reasons why and for instructions on how to adapt any printed instructions you may have that are given for straight needles, see Circular Needles under NEEDLES.

MEASUREMENTS AND GAUGE: Take your measurements or the measurements

Classic round-neck sweater with long set-in sleeves

of the person for whom you are knitting this sweater (see MEASURING THE BODY). It is very important that the measurements be accurate. Knit up a GAUGE in the yarn you plan to use.

For this example, we will assume the gauge is 4 stitches to the inch and the bust or chest measurement is 36 inches. (You must change these figures according to your gauge and measurements.) To find the number of stitches needed, multiply 4 stitches to the inch by 36 inches (144). Allow 1 inch (4 more stitches) for the tighter tension that usually results when knitting on circular needles. In this example, therefore, you would cast on 148 stitches.

RIBBING: Use a needle two sizes smaller than the one used to make your gauge, so that the ribbing you are about to knit fits tightly against the body, but cast on using a larger needle to make sure that the ribbed band will stretch enough to pull over the shoulder. Knit 1, purl 1 in ribbing for 2 inches (or the length you like). Knit one row around on the smaller needle to hold the ribbing in place. (For instructions on how to make a flat unribbed edge at the bottom of the sweater, see Two-piece Dresses under DRESSES.)

BODY: Knit the next round with the needle used to make the gauge and continue knitting until you have 11 inches, including the 2-inch ribbing. Assuming 4 stitches to the inch and allowing 2 inches at each underarm (1 inch at the front of the underarm and 1 inch at the back), cast off 8 stitches for each underarm. To do this, knit 66 stitches (these are for the front), cast off 8 stitches (front and back underarm), and knit 66 stitches (back). Turn the garment and, with the wrong (purl) side facing you, purl back on the 66 stitches (back). Turn with right side facing.

BACK: You have made the back 1 inch narrower on each side when you cast off

for the underarm. Let us assume that the measurement across the back is 14 inches from shoulder to shoulder. (To see how to take this measurement, see MEASURING THE BODY.) Yet the 66 stitches in the back measure 16½ inches. So you have to narrow the back an additional 2½ inches to make it fit in the shoulders. Half of this 2½ inches (1¼ inches) will be decreased on one side of the back at the armhole and the other half on the other side at the armhole.

With your gauge of 4 stitches to the inch, 5 stitches equals 1¼ inches. Therefore, decrease 1 stitch each side of the back *every knit row* 5 times. To decrease, at the beginning of the row slip the first stitch, knit the next stitch, and pass the slip stitch over the knit stitch. Knit up to the last 2 stitches and knit them together. Work armhole 7½ inches from cast-off stitches. This measurement is made at right angles to cast-off stitches (see MEASURING KNITTING.) *Do not measure* along armhole edge.

Your shoulder should measure 4 inches across. With 4 stitches to the inch, this would mean 16 stitches for your shoulder. Since the back of the neck is at a slightly higher level than the shoulders, don't cast off all 16 stitches at one time; the shoulders need to be tapered to the neck. Instead, cast off 8 stitches at the beginning of every row (beginning of knit row, finish row, turn, then beginning of purl row) for 4 rows. When casting off, slip the first stitch instead of knitting it. Cast off the remaining stitches very loosely (such as with a larger needle) or place stitches on a stitch hold-

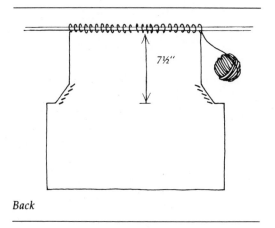

Back

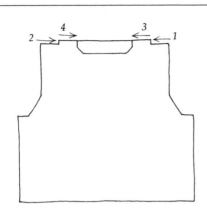

Casting off shoulder

er until you are ready to pick up for the neck band. This finishes the back of your sweater.

Remember: When casting off for a shoulder, cast off from the beginning of the row going *toward* the neck. Never cast off a shoulder at the end of a row. FRONT: Repeat the armhole shaping you did on the back by decreasing 1 stitch each side every knit row, 5 times. Work the armhole until it is 2 inches shorter than the back (5½ inches). The shaping for the front of the neck begins at a lower point than did the shaping for the back.

You need 16 stitches for your shoulder and you want a crew neck. To do this you round the neck, going from the neck to the shoulder. Allowing 3 stitches for this shaping (from the base of the neck to the shoulder), knit 19 stitches. With a

larger needle, cast off 18 stitches very loosely for the neck. Knit the last 19 stitches. (For round necks I find it preferable to slip the stitches onto a stitch holder rather than casting off either the front or back stitches. You can make sure the neck will fit over the head if you avoid tight casting off.)

Let us work first on the last 19 stitches, the right shoulder. Turn.

ROW 1: Purl back. Turn.
ROW 2: Slip 1, knit 1, pass slip stitch over knit stitch, knit the rest of the row. Turn.

Repeat rows 1 and 2 twice. You now have 16 stitches for your shoulder and a nicely curved neck. Work on the 16 stitches until they are the same length as the back to top of shoulder. Cast off 8 stitches from armhole (purl) side, going toward the neck, every other row, 2 times. Break your yarn.

With purl side facing you, connect yarn at the neck edge of the left shoulder and shape as you shaped the other shoulder, decreasing at the end of every knit row by knitting 2 stitches together 3 times. Work even until piece is the same length as the right shoulder. Cast off 8 stitches from armhole (knit) side, going toward the neck, every other row, 2 times.

CREW NECK: Before picking up ribbing for the neck, weave the left shoulder together (see Shoulder Seams under WEAVING). With the back of sweater and the right side facing you, connect the yarn at the beginning of the cast-off stitches at the neck. Using the smaller needle you used for the ribbing, pick up 1 stitch in each of the cast-off stitches by going into the front part of the cast-off stitch only. (If you've put the stitches on a stitch holder, just knit across.) Pick up the number of stitches equal to 2 inches down the left side of the neck up to the cast-off stitches on the front of the neck. Pick up 1 stitch in each of the cast-off stitches on the front. (Or, if you've used a stitch holder, knit across the stitches.) Pick up the same number of stitches on the right side of the neck as you did on the left side. Then knit 1, purl 1 in ribbing for approximately 1 inch. Cast off all stitches loosely. Leave a piece of yarn at least 10 inches long for weaving the right shoulder seam. Thread this yarn into a yarn needle and weave the 1 inch of ribbing of the neck and the shoulder seam as you did the other shoulder. (To vary the crew neck, see suggestions under NECKLINES.)

SLEEVE: Measure the arm at its widest part and measure the length of the arm (see MEASURING THE BODY). For this example we will assume that the arm length is 18 inches. We will also assume that the wrist is 7 inches and that we are still working with a gauge of 4 stitches to the inch. To start the sleeve, cast on 28 stitches (7 inches times 4 stitches to the inch), leaving about an 18-inch length of yarn hanging at the beginning of the cast-on row. You can cast these stitches onto the same circular needle you used for the body of the sweater and work back and forth on the needle, or you can use straight needles of the same size as the needles used for the body of the

sweater. If you're not in the habit of using circular needles for knitting pieces that are not tubular (pieces you could knit on straight needles), this is a good time to try. For more about circular needles in place of straight needles, see Circular Needles under NEEDLES.

Hint: To check that the wrist will fit properly, take the ribbing from the bottom of the sweater you are working on and wrap it around your wrist (or the wrist of the person the sweater is intended for). See if the number of stitches that fit around the wrist is the same as the number you are casting on for the wrist. Make sure when you do this test that you do not pull the knitted ribbing too tightly around the wrist. Allow enough give so that the ribbing can slip off easily over the hand. Remember, there will be a seam at the wrist, and the ribbing must be loose enough to pull easily over the hand.

Knit 1, purl 1 in ribbing, using the smaller needle with which you made the ribbing at the bottom of the sweater. Work the ribbing for 1½ inches, or the length you like at the wrist. Assuming that the measurement you have taken at the widest part of the arm is 12 inches, you will need 48 stitches (12 inches times 4 stitches to the inch) at this wide part. If you have knit 1½ inches of ribbing for the band at the wrist and your sleeve is to be 18 inches long to the underarm, you have 16½ inches to work for the rest of the sleeve, and the shaping from the wrist to the widest part of the arm is made in these 16½ inches.

Considering that in our example the

wrist has 28 stitches, and 48 stitches are required for the width at the top of the sleeve, you must add 20 stitches to the sleeve. It is preferable to add the stitches gradually by adding 2 stitches per row (1 stitch on each side) 10 times. Divide 16½ inches by 10. You can see that if you increase 1 stitch each side (2 per row) every 1½ inches, 10 times, this will bring the sleeve to 16½ inches and you will have your required 48 stitches. But you won't have your required length of 18 inches. Since the sleeve needs to be 18 inches from the base of the ribbing to the underarm, you will need to work 1½ inches straight (that is, with no increasing), after you've made the required increases.

Now you must shape the cap of the sleeve to make it fit the armhole. Since the sleeve at its widest part is 12 inches and the armhole is 7½ inches long—which makes 15 inches, adding back and front armholes together—something obviously has to be done to make it fit.

First, cast off 4 stitches at the beginning of each of the next 2 rows (this will match the cast-off stitches at the underarm of the body of the sweater); 34 stitches remain. Decrease 1 stitch each side every knit row 5 times; 24 stitches remain. (This will match the armhole decreasing on both the back and the front.) Next, decrease 1 stitch each side every fourth row for 2 inches; repeat 4 more times; 10 stitches remain. Cast off these remaining stitches very loosely. You now have a cap on your sleeve which will fit into your armhole.
FINISHING: Pick up the 18-inch piece of yarn you left on the sleeve. (If you do not have a piece of yarn here, take a length of yarn about 18 inches long and attach it to the first stitch.) If you have knitted the sweater with yarn that is not smooth (such as a bouclé), see Yarn for Sewing Seams or Weaving under WEAVING for suggestions for yarn substitutes.

Thread a yarn needle with the yarn for sewing and start weaving the sleeve. Sew from the right side up to the underarm. Sew from the center of the cast-off stitches at the underarm. To sew the cast-off stitches of the body and the sleeve together, follow the method described under Shoulder Seams at WEAVING. Make sure you pick up the outside (front part) of the cast-off stitches first from the body, then from the sleeve. Sew the sleeve in, weaving from one part to the other until you are back to the starting point. Sew in the other sleeve.

Side-to-Side Knit Sweater (Vertically Knit Sweater)

A sweater worked from side to side is worked all in one piece. Any stitch can

Sweater knit from side to side

be used. The sweater described here is worked in the garter stitch.

FIRST SLEEVE: You start with the sleeve. Vertically knitted sweaters (sweaters knitted from side to side) fit best when the sleeve is not tight, because there is no shaping, so allow at least 15 inches for the width at the top of the sleeve.

Take your measurements (see MEASURING THE BODY) and work up a GAUGE swatch in the yarn you plan to use. Let us say your gauge is 9 stitches to 2 inches (4½ stitches to the inch) and 10 rows to the inch. For a sleeve 15 inches wide, cast on 68 stitches (15 times 4½, or 67½, rounded to 68). Work the sleeve in the garter stitch for 2 inches less than the desired length, allowing 1 inch for stretching in blocking. These directions produce a sleeve with a loose open end, as shown in the drawing. If you want a ribbed band at the wrist, deduct 1 inch more from the length of the sleeve. Directions for the ribbed band are found toward the end of this section, under Sleeves.

FIRST SHOULDER: Add on the stitches that make up the back and the front. You need 8½ inches on each side of the sleeve for the back and front; this is the length from the base of the sleeve to the waist. Add on 39 stitches at the end of one row for the back (8½ times 4½ stitches to the inch, or approximately 39 stitches). Place a piece of colored yarn at this end. Turn. Knit back across the row and add on another 39 stitches at the end of the row for the front. You now have 146 stitches.

Work in the garter stitch for 4 inches.

You have worked the shoulder.

BACK: Finish at the end where you placed the colored yarn. This is designated the back of the sweater. Now knit 73 stitches. Put the remaining stitches on a stitch holder or a separate piece of yarn. Work on the 73 stitches for 6½ inches. You are knitting across the back of the neck. Place these 73 stitches on a second stitch holder or on a piece of yarn.

FRONT: Pick up the 73 stitches you placed on the first stitch holder. Connect the yarn at the point where you stopped knitting. Cast off 7 stitches (about 1½ inches) for the side slope of the neck. Work for 7 inches. You are now knitting across the front of the neck.

Cast on 7 stitches (about 1½ inches) for the other side of the neck slope. The number of stitches cast on at this side of the neck must be the same as the number of stitches you cast off at the other side of the neck. Then pick up the stitches from the second stitch holder with the needle going toward the neck.

SECOND SHOULDER: You have 146 stitches on the needle again. Continue knitting across the entire row for 4 inches.

SECOND SLEEVE: Cast off 39 stitches at the beginning of each of the next 2 rows. You are now finished with the body and are working on the second sleeve. Work the same number of inches as the first sleeve. Since you are using the garter stitch, the easiest way to do this is to count the ridges on the first sleeve (two rows make a ridge), knitting the same number of ridges in the second sleeve that you knitted in the first.

FINISHING: Cast off loosely. Weave

sides and sleeves together. You have a garment that extends to the waist. Will this be the top for a skirt, forming a dress? Do you want this as a long blouse? Or do you want a sweater top? We will take them one at a time.

Top of a Skirt Pin the sweater you have just knitted to the skirt with the right sides facing (side to side, front to front, back to back). Weave the top to the skirt.

Long Blouse Decide how far below the waist you want the blouse to fall; say, 5 inches. Cast on 23 stitches (5 inches times 4½ stitches to the inch or 22½ stitches, rounded to 23). Work in garter stitch for 2 inches less (10 ridges in the sample gauge) than the width of the body of the blouse. This draws in the waistline but keeps the bottom large enough to go over the shoulders, so the blouse can easily be put on. Cast off. Pin to the bottom of the blouse and weave.

Sweater-style Top Here you must decide how deep a rib you want and the style of the rib (i.e., knit 1, purl 1, or knit 2, purl 2 or knit 2, purl 1). Using a needle at least one size smaller than you used for the body of the sweater, and holding the sweater with one seam in your left hand, connect your yarn at the seam. If your gauge has held and your measurements are correct, you have between 145 and 150 ridges around the body of your sweater. Using your needle and the yarn you just connected, pick up one stitch in the ridge made by the garter stitch, skipping approximately 16 ridges, so you have approximately 130 to 136 stitches on needle. Work the ribbing

you like best for the depth you want. Cast off loosely following the stitches in the ribbing. *Remember,* "loosely" is an important word. The sweater must pass over your shoulders, and your shoulders are wider than your waist.

Sleeves Here again you must decide whether to leave the sleeve loose or knit a ribbed band on it. If you want a rib, pick up 1 stitch in every second stitch and work a 1-inch rib. If you have made a ribbed border at the bottom of the sweater, match the ribbing in the band at the sleeve to the ribbing in the bottom of the sweater.

Neck The neck as shaped can be completed as a crew neck, a turtleneck, or a jewel neckline, or it can be turned back into a collar.

CREW NECK: Take the back of the sweater. With the right side facing you, connect the yarn at the right side of the neck. With a needle at least one size smaller than the one you used to knit the sweater, pick up the stitches by going into the ridges. Pick up 28 stitches along the back of the neck (approximately 6–7 inches). Then pick up 7 stitches (1½ inches) along the side of the neck, 36 stitches (approximately 8 inches) around the front of the neck, and 7 stitches on the right side of the neck. This can be done on a 16-inch circular needle, or you can work with four double-pointed needles, dividing your stitches on three needles and working with the fourth. Either way, you will finish with a seamless neck band. Or you can pick these stitches up with straight needles. Working back and forth in this small area on straight needles will be a struggle, but it can be done.

Work in ribbing for 1 inch, matching the ribbing on the sleeve or bottom of the sweater, if you have put ribbing there. Cast off loosely. If you have worked on straight needles, sew the 1-inch seam.

TURTLENECK: Pick up stitches and work the same as for the crew neck for 2 inches. Change to the needle used for the body of the sweater and continue for 5 to 7 inches or more, depending on how deep a turtleneck you want. Cast off.

JEWEL NECKLINE: Pick up stitches the same as you did for the crew neck. Work in the stockinette stitch for 1 inch. Purl 1 row on knit side. Work the stockinette stitch for 1 row less than 1 inch. Cast off very loosely. Fold on the purl row so that the purl row is at the top of the neckband. Weave to neckline where you picked up the stitches.

Cardigan Sweater See CARDIGAN

Tape Measure

See under EQUIPMENT

Tassels

Cut a piece of cardboard 2 inches wide and the length you want for the tassel. Wrap yarn around the cardboard until there is enough thickness for the tassel. Break the yarn so it just reaches one edge of the cardboard.

Take a length of yarn, run it under the yarn on the opposite edge of the card-board, and tie securely. (You will use this length of yarn to attach the tassel to the item you are knitting.)

Take a pair of scissors and cut through the yarn along the edge of the cardboard where the yarn you have wrapped ends, the edge opposite the one where you have just tied the yarn together. Remove the cardboard.

Fold the tassel down so that you have two equal lengths tied together at the top. Take another length of yarn and wrap it around the tassel about ½ inch from the fold. Tie this tightly, cut the loose ends, and let them hang loose.

Trim the bottom fringe of the tassel, cutting off any long ends. Attach to your knitted article.

Turtleneck

Work exactly as described for the crew neck under SWEATERS except that instead of knitting 1 inch of ribbing, you contin-

Sweater with turtleneck

ue for 6 to 8 inches, depending on how deep a turtleneck you like.

This makes a close-fitting turtleneck. If you like a fuller turtleneck, work the first 1½ inches of ribbing on a smaller needle than the one you used for the rest of the sweater. Then change to a needle one to two sizes larger. Continue the ribbing on the larger needles until the turtleneck is as long as you wish.

V Neckline

The bottom of a V in a V neckline can begin as far down the front of the sweater or dress top as you like. The most important part of making a V neckline is getting as straight a line as possible from the base of the V to the shoulder.

Before you start making the V, you need to know how many stitches there are to be in the shoulder so that you know how many stitches to decrease from the bottom of the V to the shoulder. A finished garment that has a sleeve usually has a 4-inch shoulder seam. A sleeveless top will have a 3-inch shoulder to allow for the border that is usually added around the armhole. There can be a border or edge around the neckline itself; for this discussion we will assume that you will be knitting a 1-inch border

Sleeveless sweater with V neckline

around the finished neckline. Allowing for this 1-inch border, the number of stitches you need at the shoulder for a top with sleeves equals 3 inches and for a top without sleeves and a 1-inch border around the armhole 2 inches.

For this example we will assume you

have a gauge of 4 stitches to the inch and 9 rows to 2 inches (4½ rows to the inch). We will also assume that the V starts at a point 1 inch below the armhole. We will work with 74 stitches for the front of the top, the number of stitches you would have on your needle for a size 36 top using yarn and needles that give this gauge.

We now have to calculate the number of decreases necessary to make a V neckline with straight sides. You must remember that not only are you decreasing stitches for the V, you are decreasing stitches for the shaping of the armhole at the same time, and this decreasing for the armhole must be considered in your calculations. (If you are making a V neckline in a top where the armhole is not shaped, such as one with a dropped shoulder, you of course do not have to figure in the stitches decreased for the armhole shaping, since there are none.)

To begin your calculations, you must know how many stitches there are in each half of the front. In this example, there are 37 stitches for each half of the front since there are 74 stitches for the front before the armhole shaping. If you are working with an odd number of stitches for the front, subtract 1 stitch in your calculations and, when dividing the stitches as you work, place that center stitch on a safety pin until you are ready to make the border of the neckline.

You are starting your V 1 inch below the armhole, and the armhole, for this example, begins 8½ inches below the shoulder. So, you will be making your decreases over a total of 9½ inches. With

a gauge of 9 rows to 2 inches, or 4½ rows to the inch, this means that the decreases for the V are to be made over 42¾ rows. For our figures we will use 42 rows.

Remember that you are casting off stitches to shape the armhole. Assuming that you are doing the usual shaping for a set-in sleeve, you cast off 1 inch (4 stitches) for each armhole, or a total of 8 stitches for the entire front. Subtract these 4 stitches from the 37 you have for each half of the front. This leaves 33 stitches on your needle for each half after casting off for the armhole. Remember that you will also be decreasing for shaping of the armhole, usually 1 stitch at the armhole every knit row 5 times. This will leave 28 stitches on each half.

Now we can determine where to make the decreases for the V shape. You need 12 stitches at the shoulder for a sweater with sleeves, and you have 28 stitches for each half. You have to decrease 16 stitches. These decreases must be evenly spaced over the distance from the base of the V to the shoulder so that the sides of the V are straight.

It is best to make the decreases on a knit row. Since you cannot divide 42 rows (the number of rows where the increases are to be made) evenly by 16 (the number of stitches to be decreased), a way to decrease for a straight V is to space the decreases farther apart toward the bottom of the V and closer together toward the top. For this example, space the decreases every fourth row for the first 20 rows. This makes 10 decreases. Then decrease the 6 stitches that remain to be decreased every other row over 11 rows.

Border

Measure the side of the V. For this measurement, place the tape measure at the place where you have cast off for the shoulder on the neckline side (not the armhole side). Measure to the base of the V. This measurement is usually at least 1 inch longer than the depth from the underarm to the shoulder, the measurement used to calculate the decreases needed to make the V. You can make a border in ribbing or in stockinette stitch. In either case, make a gauge in the stitch you have chosen using a needle one or two sizes smaller than the one you used for knitting the top. Now calculate the number of stitches you have to pick up along the edge of the V. To do this, multiply the number of inches in the length of one side of the V times the number of stitches you get to the inch in your gauge.

To make the border, use the needle you used to make the gauge for the border. With the right side of your sweater or top facing you, connect the yarn to the back of the neck at the right corner. Place the needle in the front loop of the first cast-off stitch and pull the yarn through. Continuing in this way, pick up a stitch in each of the cast-off stitches across the back of the neck. Pick up the stitches along the left front of the V (see illustration at CARDIGANS for picking up stitches along a border). If you placed a center stitch on a safety pin before because you had an odd number of stitches in the front, pick it up now. Continue by picking up the same number of stitches along the right front as you did along the left front.

In making the border, you decrease at the base of the V so that the border lies flat. Place a marker between the center stitch at the base of the V. If you have an odd number of stitches, mark the center stitch at the base of the V with a piece of yarn or a ring marker and knit this stitch every row. Do not include it in the decreasing.

Using either a ribbing stitch (knit 1, purl 1) or a stockinette stitch, make a border by working 1 inch and, at the same time, decreasing at the base of the V. If you are working on circular needles, decrease before the marker by slipping 1 stitch, knitting the next stitch, and passing the slip stitch over the knit stitch, and then knit 2 stitches together after the marker. If you are working back and forth on straight needles, follow the decreasing as just described for the knit row and purl 2 together on the purl row, working from the back of the loop after the marker.

Work a 1-inch border, making the decreases on every row. Cast off loosely.

To make a stockinette stitch border with a facing, purl 1 row on the knit side instead of casting off the last row. This is the turning edge of the border. Knit the same number of rows for the facing that you knitted for the border, increasing where you decreased on the other side. Then cast off. Turn back on the purl row and sew the facing in place.

Remember: When decreasing for the V,

in order to make the decreases slant away from the center, decrease the stitches on the right front by knitting 2 stitches together; when decreasing the stitches for the left front, work by slipping 1 stitch, knitting the next stitch, and passing the slip stitch over the knit stitch.

Vertical Knitting

See SIDE-TO-SIDE KNITTING

Waistbands

Although there are a number of ways to
make waistbands for skirts and for those
one-piece dresses that have waistbands, I
prefer a knitted waistband into which
elastic is inserted. This waistband is
made after the skirt or other garment is
cast off the needles.

Knitted Casing

To make a waistband, take the circular
needle used to knit the skirt and pick up
the front half of each cast-off stitch at
the top of the skirt. Knit the first row by
knitting all the stitches from the back.
Knit 1 inch the regular way, using knit
stitches only. Then purl 1 row. This row
is the top of the waistband. Knit until
you have 1 row less than the number of
rows in the first inch knitted and cast off

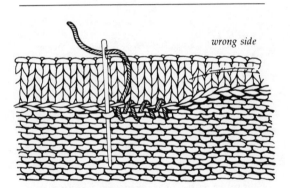

wrong side

Weaving waistband in place

loosely. Break the yarn about 1 yard
from the last stitch.

Fold the waistband back on the purl
row and weave the cast-off stitches onto

the garment top with the yard of yarn left hanging. Sew the waistband down, leaving a ½-inch opening to run elastic through (see Elastic below). After the elastic is inserted, sew down the ½-inch opening. Finish the top of the waistband with a row of crocheted slip stitches (see SLIP STITCHES) loosely worked in the purl stitch of the turned edge, going into the front of the purl stitch as you work.

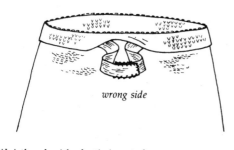

wrong side

Waistband with elastic inserted

Rickrack or Herringbone Casing

Made with a Yarn Needle   Measure elastic to size required, adding 2 inches for overlap. Fold the elastic in half, allowing for a 1-inch overlap at each end, and place a pin at the fold. Fold again and mark the elastic in quarter sections. Mark the top edge of the skirt in quarters in the same way. Matching the pins in the elastic to those in the skirt, pin the elastic to the skirt on the inside. Hold the top of the skirt in your left hand. Thread a yarn needle with yarn and connect the yarn to the skirt below the edge of the elastic. Bring the yarn over the elastic at an angle slightly to the left and insert the yarn needle through the top of the elastic and through the top edge of the skirt. Pull the yarn through and insert the needle in the skirt stitch directly below the elastic. Pull through and again insert the needle through the elastic and the top of the skirt, about ½ inch to the left of the last stitch taken on the top edge. Continue in this manner until the elastic is attached to the skirt. Sew the ends of the elastic together.

Made with a Crochet Hook   Measure the width of the elastic. Let us say that it measures ¾ inch. Connect the yarn to the top of the skirt at the point where the bottom of the elastic will fall. In this example, that point would be ¾ inch from the top edge of the skirt. Crochet a chain about ¾ inch long. Holding the chain about ½ inch to the left of where you connected the yarn, attach it to the top edge of the skirt with a slip stitch. Chain another ¾-inch length and slip-stitch it to the lower edge of where the elastic will fall and at a point ½ inch to the left. Continue around the skirt. Run the elastic, measured to the desired length (see below under Elastic), under the crocheted mesh, overlap the ends, and sew them together.

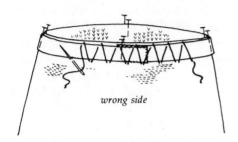

Rickrack casing for elastic made with yarn needle

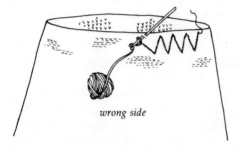

Rickrack casing for elastic made with crochet hook

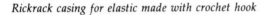

Elastic

Buy ¾-inch elastic in black or white. Use white elastic for lighter color yarns and black for darker ones. Check how the yarn you are using is to be cleaned—that is, machine washed or dry cleaned—and then make sure the elastic you buy can be cleaned by that method.

To complete the waistband, cut the elastic 1 to 1½ inches longer than your waistline measurement. Run the elastic through the waistband, overlap it 2 inches, and sew it together. If you gain some weight and the band does not feel comfortable but the skirt (or other knit) still fits, just open up the elastic and resew it with less of an overlap.

Washing

Natural Yarn

Knitted garments of natural yarns can be kept for ages if properly cared for. You can have them dry cleaned, but it's worth taking a little time to wash them. They will look fresher and probably last longer.

Fill your basin with soap flakes and warm water. *Do not* use strong soaps, detergents, or hot water. These will ruin your garment. *Do not* allow the garment to soak. Just squeeze the sudsy water through the garment. *Do not* rub. Let the water run out, squeezing the garment against the wall of the basin to get as much water out of it as possible. Repeat the entire process a second time, moving the garment around with your hands, squeezing it to allow the sudsy water to go through the garment. Then put fresh water in the basin with just a pinch of soap flakes and rinse in the slightly soapy water. The soap flakes keep the yarn fluffy and new. Drain the water, squeezing the garment against the basin until you get out as much water as possible. *Do not* wring out the garment.

When you feel you have all the water

out that can be squeezed, put the garment all bunched together on a terry towel and roll it up. Let it sit long enough for the towel to absorb the excess moisture, about an hour.

Now lay the garment out on a fresh towel to its proper size, checking the measurements, just the way you want it to look when dry. Make sure the fronts are even, the armholes flat, the shoulders the width you want, the chest measurement and hip measurements correct. Make sure that the garment is not stretched in length or shrunk and that the sleeves are the correct length. Allow it to dry in the shade. Sun and radiators will harm the yarn. *Never* hang a garment on a hanger or bar when it is still wet. Natural yarns do not have to be blocked after washing.

Synthetic Yarn

It is wise to keep at least one label from each knitted piece you make. Mark the color on the inside of the label and wash according to the instructions on the label.

Combinations of Natural and Synthetic Yarns

Follow the method described under Synthetic Yarn.

Weaving

Weaving, as the term is used in this book, is a way of joining parts of a garment together. It is preferable to cro-

cheting a seam or sewing it with a back stitch because weaving produces a flat rather than a bulky seam, does not decrease the width of the knitted garment by putting some of the knitted stitches in the seam, and allows the garment to be worn on both sides if the stitch used to make the garment is a reversible one.

The first stitch on every other row appears as a nub or bump on each edge of the knitted piece. Pieces woven together should match exactly; that is, have the same number of nubs. You can be sure of this by counting the nubs along the sides of the pieces.

To weave two parts together, place the right sides together facing you and use a yarn or darning needle. The yarn end left over when the first row was cast on should be used for weaving the pieces together. If there isn't enough yarn to sew the entire seam, sew as much as you can; then add another piece of yarn to finish the seam. If you have only a few inches of yarn in the yarn end to sew with, thread a new piece of yarn in the yarn needle and tie it to the beginning of the seam. Weaving is difficult with very bulky yarn or with yarn that has slubs or bumps. For these yarns use a heavy cotton sewing thread or a matching tapestry wool for the sewing yarn. For more hints about yarn for weaving see Yarn for Sewing Seams or Weaving at the end of this section.

With the needle held in the center space between the two parts to be woven, go into the nub on the right piece from below. Then put the needle into the center of the nub of the left piece from below. It is like lacing a shoe. Continue to the end of the seam.

Weaving a seam

Smooth out the seam and adjust the tension by loosening the sewing yarn if you have pulled it too tight or pulling the yarn tighter if there are gaps between the stitches. Tie it off. See Cleaning Up Ends under FINISHING for what to do with loose yarn ends.

If you don't like to weave or sew seams, you can eliminate seams entirely by using circular needles, but you'll have to sew your sleeve seams. (Some knitters prefer to avoid sewing sleeve seams by knitting sleeves on small circular needles or on four needles, starting at the top of the sleeve and decreasing down to the cuff. I do not recommend this method.) See Circular Needles under NEEDLES.

Shoulder Seams

The usual instructions for shaping shoulders on garments call for casting off a number of stitches at the beginning of a number of rows. Typical instructions will say: Cast off 5 stitches at the beginning of the next 4 rows. This will give you two steps of 5 stitches each on each side of your knitted piece.

Instead of knitting the first stitch of each step when casting off, try slipping it instead. This eliminates the bump at the beginning of each step, gives the shoulder a smoother look, and makes it easier to sew the shoulder parts together.

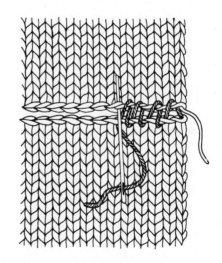

Weaving a shoulder seam

For the sewing of the shoulder seam, use a tapestry or wool needle and the yarn left from casting off. Start sewing at the neck edge with the right side of the work facing you. Starting from the center space, go into the outer edge of the stitch of the back shoulder in an outward direction. Your needle is always coming from the center out. Then put your needle into the outer stitch of the front of the garment going from the center space outward. Continue this up to the last stitch of the step. You have now reached the first step on the shoulder. Place the needle into the outside of the last stitch of the step and then into the first stitch of the step below. Repeat this on the other side. Continue sewing to the end of the shoulder. Do not pull the yarn too

tightly or you will make the shoulder too narrow and the sewing thread may snap when you wear your sweater. Do not let the yarn go too lax or you will have gaps. Sewing this way, you can make a flat, smooth seam with the correct yarn tension.

If you have knitted a garment that has a reversible stitch, such as might be used in a vest or slip-on sweater, repeat this sewing procedure on the wrong side to produce a flat reversible seam. You can now wear your knitted garment on both sides.

Yarn for Sewing Seams or Weaving

Whenever possible, use the same yarn for the final weaving or sewing as you used for knitting. Where the yarn is too nubby for sewing, tangles too much, or breaks easily, substitute a heavy cotton thread or needlepoint yarn. Needlepoint yarns come in a large range of colors, and you can almost always match your yarn. Do not use a shiny yarn to sew a garment made of a dull-finish yarn. You can sometimes use a dull-finish yarn with a shiny yarn, but I recommend matching the type of sewing yarn with the type of yarn in the knitted piece.

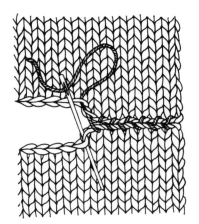

Weaving together the "steps" in the shoulder

Widening Knits

See ALTERING

Yarn

Pick a yarn you will be happy working on. If it feels uncomfortable in the skein, you won't enjoy working with it. Many yarn shops and department stores carry samples of their yarns worked up into swatches. Ask to see these samples before buying your yarn, since yarn looks very different knitted than when it is wound into a ball or twisted into a skein.

Try experimenting with yarns. Mix them together. Mohair goes well with tweeds and linens. Try mixing thick and thin yarns. Create your own tweeds by mixing colors. The possible combinations are limited only by your imagination.

Ply

The number of strands that have been put together to make up the yarn is indicated by the ply number. A 3-ply yarn is made of 3 strands of yarn, a 4-ply yarn, 4 strands, and so on. The strands can be loosely twisted, braided, or combined in other ways. The way they are combined affects the way the knitted stitch will look. Keep this in mind when substituting one yarn of comparable weight and thickness for another.

You might think that a 4-ply yarn is thicker than a 3-ply yarn. Not necessarily so. A 3-ply yarn can be very fine or very thick, depending on the individual strands used. When substituting one yarn for another, you cannot consider that yarns of the same ply are interchangeable. You must consider the yarn's thickness and how it knits up. See Substituting Yarns, later in this section.

Dye Lot

All the yarn that is dyed together will have the same dye lot number, and this number is usually printed on the label. Make sure that all the skeins you buy for your project have the same dye lot number. Buy one or two extra balls or skeins of yarn. You might later decide to lengthen the garment, change the sleeve, or add a turtleneck or hood. It would be difficult to match the dye lot.

However, if you run short, try to match the closest color you can. If you have two different dye lots in the same color yarn but can see little or no variance, you can use the yarn if you work as follows:

Work until you have about 6 rows of the old yarn left. Work 1 row with the original yarn. Work 1 row with the new yarn. Work 1 row with the original yarn. Work 2 rows with the new yarn. Work 1 row with the original yarn. Finish work with the new yarn.

Weight

Years ago there were three basic yarn weights, and older knitting magazines and instruction books you might have will mention them by name: baby yarn, sports yarn, and worsted. Baby yarn is a fine yarn, usually 2 to 4 ply. Yarns for socks, gloves, and some sweaters, medium-weight yarns, are sports yarn. And heavy yarn, usually a 4-ply yarn, is called worsted. Although these terms are still used, yarns available today are so varied that they do not readily fall into these old categories.

Types

You can buy yarns of wool, cotton, rayon, linen, nylon, orlon, polyester, metal, other natural fibers, other synthetic fibers, or in combinations of one or more types. It is very important to keep one label from the yarn you are using. Consult the label before washing or dry cleaning the garment.

Here is a list of yarns commonly available. There are many others, and new blends are being made every day.

Alpaca comes from the fleece of the alpaca, an animal that lives in the high altitudes of the Andes mountains, mostly in Peru. The yarn comes in a lightweight 3-ply yarn and a heavier 4-ply yarn.
Angora comes from the specially raised Angora rabbit. It is blended with other fibers to achieve a soft furry look.
Berber yarns come from the sheep of the Berber tribes of Africa. It is a rugged yarn with irregular flecks of darker colors running through.
Blended yarns are made of two or more fibers which are mixed before spinning.
Bouclé is a novelty twisted yarn and creates a rough or looped surface. It is a stretchy yarn and is made of a variety of fibers.
Brushed wools are yarns with a downy nap that is brushed up after knitting to raise the nap.
Camel's hair is a soft, strong yarn made from the hair of camels.
Cashmere comes from the Cashmere goat that lives in the high mountains of central Asia. It is one of the finest, richest, and most expensive yarns. Cashmere is sometimes available unblended, but it is more often sold blended with lamb's wool.

Chenille is a yarn with a pile coming out at right angles from the center strand. It is usually made of cotton, wool, or rayon.

Icelandic wool comes from Icelandic sheep. It has long glossy fibers and is a water-repellent and wind-resistant yarn, light in weight and very soft.

Lamb's wool comes from lambs only seven to nine months old and is the first shearing of the young sheep.

Marl yarn is made by twisting two or more strands of different colors.

Merino wool is from the Spanish merino sheep. It is soft, fine, and strong.

Mohair is from the fleece of the Angora goat and has a soft and silky texture. After mohair is knitted, it can be brushed with a brush that has plastic bristles, or the nap can be raised with a hair pick pulled lightly across the surface.

Shetland yarns are from sheep grown on the Shetland Isles and nearby mainland Scotland. This wool is durable and resilient.

Thick and thin yarn is spun to create an irregular, nubby effect. It can be blended of any kind of yarn.

Virgin wool is natural wool, spun for the first time into yarn.

Wool comes from wool-bearing animals, especially the sheep. The yarn ranges from very soft to coarse and rough.

Woolen yarn is spun of different-length short fibers that are crisscrossed at irregular places.

Substituting Yarn

You cannot always find the yarn called for in the instructions, or you may not be able to afford it. You can substitute a similar yarn in a similar weight, but remember that the garment might have a different look because the yarn you are using might not have the same twist or texture as the original. This does not mean that your garment will not look as good. It might even look better than the garment made of the original yarn. Ask to see a knitted swatch of the yarn you are substituting or, if possible, work up a swatch yourself.

When substituting yarn, you *must* check the gauge of the new yarn. Work up a gauge swatch (see GAUGE) and adjust your needles until you get the same number of rows and stitches to the inch as called for in your instructions.

If you are not substituting a similar yarn but want to try the knitted garment in a thinner yarn, you can still get the number of stitches to the inch you need, but you'll have to use a larger needle. Even though you get the correct number of stitches to the inch with the larger needle, you might not get the exact number of rows to the inch you need. If this happens, you must be sure to measure all your lengths by inches, not by rows. For example, if your instructions tell you to work even for 6 rows, look at the gauge given in the instructions and find out how many *inches* 6 rows is equal to. Then knit for the required number of inches instead.

If the yarn you chose is even a little heavier than that called for in the instructions, you will have the same problem in reverse; that is, you might get the proper number of stitches to the inch by using a smaller needle, but you will get fewer rows to the inch. You still need to measure lengths for the garment to come out correctly.

If you want to use yarn much thinner or thicker than that called for, you will have to change the gauge and calculate the number of stitches you need. If the yarn you choose is much thinner and the needles you need are much larger than those called for, the garment will turn out very loosely knitted and will stretch easily. If the yarn you choose is much thicker and you use a much smaller needle to get the gauge called for, the garment when finished will be too tightly knit and will not fall properly. In either case, you will not be happy with the finished product.

Here's how to change the gauge and find out the number of stitches you need for the yarn you like. Look in the instructions for the number of stitches you would cast on if you were using the yarn called for. Divide this number by the number of stitches per inch in the gauge. This will tell you the number of *inches* you are casting on. Make up a new gauge using the yarn you prefer. Find out the gauge you are getting for this new yarn; that is, the number of stitches to the inch (see GAUGE to find out how to do this).

Take the number of stitches to the inch in the new gauge and multiply it by the number of inches your instructions tell you to cast on (the number you just determined). You now know the

new number of stitches you need to cast on, using your new yarn and needles. Then adjust the rest of the instructions accordingly. For example, if you are making a sweater, look at the directions for casting off the stitches at the underarm. If the instructions tell you to cast off 6 stitches and the original gauge was 4 stitches to an inch, you know that you have to cast off the equivalent in your new gauge of 1½ inches. Translate all directions in the instructions this way.

Reusing Yarn

You have ripped a garment you did not like but love the yarn it was made of. Or you are shortening or restyling it. Don't knit with the ripped yarn until you have straightened out the ripple. Wind the used yarn around the back of a chair into skeins that are not too large. Then, either: (1) dampen the yarn (do not soak it), pull it out to eliminate the ripple, and hang it from a bar in your shower or from the shower head until it is dry, or (2) hold the yarn stretched out in front of steaming water and move it back and forth until the ripple is removed.

If the garment or other knitted piece that you ripped was soiled, I suggest washing the yarn, following the instructions under WASHING. Before washing, tie the skein every few inches with pieces of the same yarn to prevent tangling.

If the garment was knitted recently and you decide you do not like it, just rip it out. You may find that the yarn has not rippled and that it is not necessary to do anything but reknit.

Be prepared to lose some yarn in the ripping. When you figure your next knitting project, make sure you take this into account.

Winding Up a Ball of Yarn

Yarn sold in skeins or hanks is often tied at regular intervals to prevent tangling. Do not remove any of these ties until you are ready to wind the yarn. First, place the skein on someone's out-stretched hands or on the back of a chair so that the skein forms a circle. You will notice that one of the ties is connected to the yarn of the skein and the rest are completely separate. Cut the separate ties. Then untie the tie that is knotted to the yarn in the skein.

Pick up one end of the yarn and begin to unwind the yarn on the skein by wrapping it around the four fingers of your hand until you have about twenty or thirty turns of yarn around your fingers. Always wind yarn over your fingers. Never wind it into a tight ball. You do not want to lose the yarn's elasticity, fluffiness, or softness. Take the yarn off your fingers and hold the ball in your hand. Continue winding the yarn around the yarn in your hand and around your fingers about the same number of times as before. Holding the yarn together, remove your fingers from the yarn ball. Repeat this process until the ball of yarn is complete.

Weights in Which Yarn Is Sold

Domestic yarns are usually sold in ounces. Imported yarns are usually sold in grams. This table will help you convert the weights you see on labels to the weights shown in instructions.

common weights of U.S. yarn	metric equivalents
1 oz	28.35 gr
4 oz	113.4 gr
8 oz	226.88 gr
1 lb	454 gr

common weights of yarn of other countries	U.S. equivalents
25 gr	0.9 oz
50 gr	1.8 oz
1 kg (1,000 gr)	2.2 lb

Yarn Conversions

If your instructions call for yarn in ounces and you are considering buying yarn sold in grams, here is a handy conversion table:

1 oz. = 25 gr. + 3.35 gr.

For 3 oz.	buy 4 balls @ 25 gr.	
	or 2 balls @ 50 gr.	
For 7 oz.	buy 8 balls @ 25 gr.	
	or 4 balls @ 50 gr.	
For 12 oz.	buy 14 balls @ 25 gr.	
	or 7 balls @ 50 gr.	
For 16 oz.	buy 18 balls @ 25 gr.	
	or 9 balls @ 50 gr.	
For 20 oz.	buy 23 balls @ 25 gr.	
	or 12 balls @ 50 gr.	

Yokes

The top part of a garment from the neckline down to the underarm can be worked in one piece in the round. This kind of top is called a yoke, and it can be made in many patterns.

Sweater with yoke

Plain Yoke

Work your sweater or other garment up to the underarm and cast off the required number of stitches at the underarm. Knit the sleeves on straight needles or work back and forth on circular needles. Work up to the underarm and cast off for the underarm, keeping the rest of the stitches on the needle. Take a circular needle of the size you used to knit the body and place all the stitches on it in the following order: front, right sleeve, back, left sleeve. You now have to calculate how to decrease evenly from this point at the underarm to the neckline.

To show you how to do this, let us use a sample gauge of 3 stitches to the inch and 4 rows to the inch. The average neckline is 16 inches. (If the neck is made smaller, the garment won't fit over the head.) Multiplying 16 inches by 3 stitches to the inch gives 48. This is the number of stitches you need at the neck. Subtract this number from the number of stitches you have on your circular needle. For this example we will assume that you have 138 stitches (39 stitches each for the front and the back and 30 stitches each for the sleeves). Subtracting the 48 stitches needed at the neck from the 138 you have on the needles tells you that you need to decrease 90 stitches in the yoke.

You now determine how many rows you have in which to make these decreases. Comfortable yokes are usually 8½ inches deep when measured at right angles to the underarm. This corresponds roughly to the armhole measurement. Multiply this yoke depth (8½ inches) by 4 rows to the inch (your gauge). This tells you that you can lose (or decrease) these 90 stitches in 34 rows. The decreasing should be gradual, but you have a few choices. You can either decrease 10 stitches 9 times or you can decrease 15 stitches 6 times. Either way would be correct.

Now let us see on which of the 34 rows you will make these decreases. If you are going to decrease 10 stitches 9 times, divide 34 by 9. This gives 3 plus 7 rows left over. The simplest way to work with these numbers is to work the decreases every third row, but start the first decrease after row 7. To do this, *work 11 stitches, then knit 2 stitches together.* Repeat between asterisks around the row. If you wish to decrease 15 stitches 6 times, divide the 34 rows of the yoke by 6. This tells you to make the 15 decreases every fifth row. Space the decreases on the decrease row as evenly as possible. To do this, *work 7 stitches, then knit 2 stitches together* around the row.

ANOTHER WAY TO MAKE THE YOKE: Decrease only ½ the stitches you plan to decrease and then change to smaller needles, knitting to the neckline and decreasing the rest of the stitches then. Start by decreasing ¼ of the stitches in the first row, work 2½ inches, and then decrease the same number of stitches again. Change to a smaller needle and work to the neckline. Figure out the gauge for the smaller needle (the number of stitches you are getting to the inch) and multiply this number by the 16 inches you need for the neck opening. Decrease to this number of stitches.

Patterned Yoke

Here is a four-row pattern that makes a lovely yoke. Remember that you are working this pattern on circular needles.

ROW 1: *Purl 4, knit 1, yarn over, knit 1*. Repeat across row.

ROW 2: *Purl 4, knit 3*. Repeat across row.

ROW 3: *Purl 4, knit 3. Place the left-hand needle into the front of the first stitch of the knit 3, lift the stitch, and drop it over the other 2 knit stitches*. Repeat across row.

ROW 4: *Purl 4, knit 2*. Repeat across row.

Let us use the same number of stitches for this example as we used before. There are 138 stitches on the circular needle. As you remember, you have 90 stitches to lose, or decrease, and 34 rows in which to lose them. Since you are working with a pattern here, you have to adjust the number of stitches being decreased so that it works evenly with the pattern. The pattern contains a multiple of 6 stitches. Change the number of decreases you need to make to a number that can be divided by 6 evenly. The number 90 fits this qualification. You want to decrease gradually. You can decrease in any combination of rows and decreases that accomplishes this. For this example we will make 4 decreases every eighth row. Here's how to make these decreases using this pattern stitch.

1. Purl 2 stitches together in the center of every purl-4 panel for 1 row. Your pattern will remain the same, but you will be doing purl 3 between the patterns.
2. Work 7 rows.
3. Decrease again by purling 2 stitches together between each pattern for 1 row. You will now have 2 purl stitches between each pattern.
4. Work 4 rows.
5. Purl 2 together in every purl-2 panel across the row. This will give you a purl stitch between panels.
6. Work until you have 8½ inches,

ending with Row 1 of the pattern.

7. On the next row *knit the purl stitch together with the first knit stitch, knit 2*. Repeat this across the row. Work 1 inch and finish the neckline.

Yoke Neckline   After completing the yoke, build up the back of the neck so that it is slightly above shoulder level by working back and forth on the back neck stitches for 2 rows. Complete the neck band, following the instructions for crew necks under the Classic Round-neck Sweater part of the SWEATERS section of this book, or just cast off loosely and finish with edging as shown under EDG-INGS.

Zippers

Before adding a zipper, sew the garment together, block it, and place it on a flat surface. Measure the length of the closing and buy a zipper ½ inch shorter than this length.

Take some of your yarn to the store and try to find a zipper as close in color as possible to the color of your yarn. Most notion stores will cut a zipper to the length you need if such a zipper is not readily available.

Pin the zipper into place ⅛ inch in from the edge of the garment. Using matching sewing thread, sew down the outer edge of the zipper to the garment. Next, do a running backstitch along the sewing lines marked on the zipper. If there are no marks on your zipper, do this stitch about ⅛ inch from the zipper teeth.